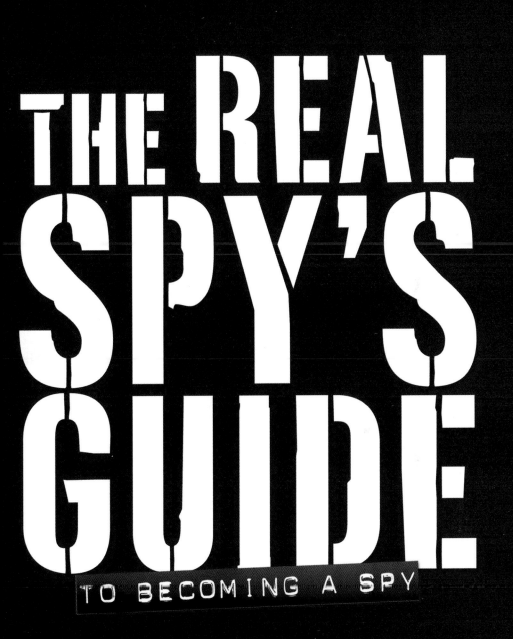

THE REAL SPY'S GUIDE

TO BECOMING A SPY

Acknowledgments

The authors would like to acknowledge the editorial assistance of Anna Slafer, Jackie Eyl, and Dr. Thomas Boghardt of the International Spy Museum's Exhibitions and Programs Department. Though never spies themselves, they each have extraordinary insight into that shadowy world and its practitioners.

All statements of fact, opinion, or analysis expressed are those of the author and do not reflect the official positions or views of the Central Intelligence Agency (CIA) or any other U.S Government agency. Nothing in the contents should be construed as asserting or implying U.S. Government authentication of information or CIA endorsement of the author's views. This material has been reviewed by the CIA to prevent the disclosure of classified information.

Library of Congress Cataloging-in-Publication Data
Earnest, Peter.
The real spy's guide to becoming a spy / by Peter Earnest and Suzanne Harper,
in association with the International Spy Museum.
p. cm.
ISBN 978-0-8109-8329-8 (Harry N. Abrams, Inc.)
1. Spies–Juvenile literature. 2. Spies–Vocational guidance–Juvenile literature.
3. Intelligence service–Juvenile literature. 4. Espionage–Juvenile literature.
I. Harper, Suzanne. II. International Spy Museum (Washington, D.C.) III. Title.

JF1525.I6.E27 2009
327.120023–dc22
2009000518

ABRAMS
THE ART OF BOOKS SINCE 1949

115 West 18th Street
New York, NY 10011
www.abramsbooks.com

THE REAL SPY'S GUIDE

TO BECOMING A SPY

BY **PETER EARNEST** WITH **SUZANNE HARPER**
IN ASSOCIATION WITH THE INTERNATIONAL SPY MUSEUM

ABRAMS BOOKS FOR YOUNG READERS
NEW YORK

Preface

and onto my tuxedo shirt as I lay on my back securing the bug into a hidden compartment in the back of the antique wooden desk. I had excused myself from my host's small dinner party and secretly stolen into his office while supposedly on my way to the bathroom. Sweating profusely and aware that he was only a room away, I quickly finished and hurried back to the party. I wiped the perspiration off my face, and brushed the small pile of wood shavings that had fallen on my shirt into a little envelope and pocketed it. The bugging operation was done, but it was a close call!

The target whose desk I had bugged was my own agent. Thankfully, he never suspected a thing. And we soon uncovered his treachery—he had been spying against us! Secret operations like this make your heart beat faster. It reminds me of when I first entered the shadowy world of agent meetings, covert operations, and secret reports.

It was during the Cold War, the forty-year-long struggle between the United States and the Soviet Union, that the Central Intelligence Agency (CIA) recruited me into its secret branch, called the Clandestine Service. Fresh out of Georgetown University and a stint in the Marine Corps, I knew nothing about the world of intelligence and spying, let alone about the CIA and its worldwide network of secret agents and covert activities. Little did I realize my life as an intelligence officer and "spy," as some call me, would become my calling for the next thirty years and take me to exciting assignments around the world.

After I left the CIA, I became the executive director of the International Spy Museum in Washington, D.C., the only such museum in the world. Here I've met fascinating visitors—authors, journalists, filmmakers, and students—all looking for a glimpse into the mysterious world of intelligence and spying. I know many of them wonder to themselves if they could be a spy. But what exactly is a "spy"?

Movies, books, and TV show us many different images of spies. Some, like James Bond, set out to save the world, while others are depicted as dark, sinister figures with evil aims. Where is the truth? The newspapers and TV regularly report on those who have betrayed their country's secrets for greed or vengeance, often at the expense of others' lives. And history bears many tales of brave individuals who, in times of war and at great risk to their own lives, engaged in the dangerous pursuit of spying for a good cause.

There have been many changes in the world since the end of the Cold War, but while the threats may be different, the need for timely and accurate intelligence to protect our country remains. The terrorist attacks against America on September 11, 2001, and the fact that more countries have nuclear weapons than ever before highlight some of the many threats our country now faces. We now live in a world where intelligence and spying are at the forefront of our country's defenses.

At times like these, many of you are looking for ways to join the world of intelligence. It is one I enjoyed and found immensely rewarding, knowing that my work helped my country stay free. But it is also a world that is complex and takes a lot of hard work to join. I hope this book will help you to understand the intelligence community better as you look for your own way to serve your country.

Peter Earnest

Executive Director of the International Spy Museum

Contents

CHAPTER 1

WHY SPY?

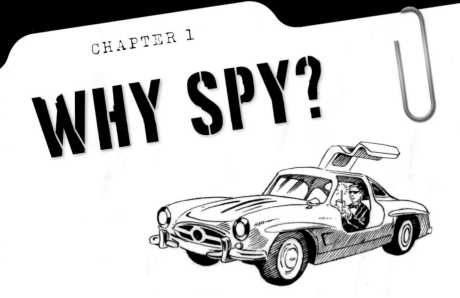

W ho hasn't dreamed of living the life of a superspy? You'd spend your time sneaking down dark streets, following a bad guy (or trying to shake that bad guy off your trail). You'd break into office buildings to steal top secret documents or computer disks. You might even hang from the ceiling like Tom Cruise in *Mission: Impossible* or race a BMW along twisting mountain roads like James Bond!

Well, here's the bad news. The only way you'll get to do any of that stuff is if you become an actor—and if you snag the role of James Bond, of course.

But here's the good news. You *can* be a spy if you want to. And although you may not live quite the glamorous life you've seen in the movies, you'll be able to do important work and serve your country. This book will tell you how.

• • •

Every year, hundreds of thousands of people visit the International Spy Museum in Washington, D.C. Perhaps it won't surprise you to know that many people, from elementary school students to grandparents, ask the same question: "Could I be a spy?"

They're curious about what the spy's life is really like. Do you have to wear disguises? Do you have to lie to your family and friends about what you do? Do you get to use cool gadgets, like the ones in the James Bond movies?

They want to know what kind of training they need before applying for a job as a spy, how to apply, and what the job interview is like. What should my major be in college? What kind of questions will I be asked by an interviewer? Will I have to take a lie detector test?

They often wonder if they have what it takes to spy. They ask themselves: Am I brave enough? Am I smart enough? Would I have to shoot a gun? Would I have to kill people?

This book will answer the most common questions people ask about becoming a spy. By the time you've finished reading it, you'll know whether you might make a good spy and what steps you should take to prepare for a career as a spy. And you'll discover many spy skills that you can practice right now to prepare yourself to become a spy someday.

HOW LONG HAVE SPIES BEEN AROUND?

Spies have been around ever since one person had a secret and someone else wanted to find it out—in other words, forever!

Here's a quick tour through some highlights in the history of spying:

- **1800 BCE:** The first recorded account of spying is carved on a clay tablet in the royal court of King Hammurabi of Babylon.

- **1200 BCE:** The Greeks, who are at war with the Trojans, offer to their gods the gift of a large wooden horse. The Trojans retrieve it and wheel it inside the city gate. That night, the Greeks—who had hidden inside the horse—sneak out and overpower their enemy. (This was a classic deception operation. Today, this kind of operation would be called a covert action.)

- **c. 500 BCE:** Sun Tzu writes *The Art of War*, the first book on war strategy, deception, and espionage.

- **1500s:** Sir Francis Walsingham creates and operates the most powerful spy ring of its time for his queen, Elizabeth I of England.

- **1778:** General George Washington creates a spy network and conducts deception operations that help the American colonists win the Revolutionary War.

1861: During the American Civil War, the Union employs private railroad detective Allan Pinkerton as a spymaster and counterintelligence officer. Also, Alexander Gardner, America's first photojournalist, spies for the Union with the help of his camera.

1862: During the American Civil War, Union forces send a hydrogen-filled balloon into the air. The balloon is equipped with a telegraph that instantly reports Confederate troop movements. This is an early example of aerial reconnaissance.

1863: Harriet Tubman creates a spy network to steal Confederate secrets during the American Civil War. Also: The Union creates the Bureau of Military Information as the first American all-source intelligence arm.

1908: The U.S. Department of Justice creates the Bureau of Information, which is renamed the Federal Bureau of Investigation (FBI) in 1935. (J. Edgar Hoover would be the longest-serving director of the Bureau, holding the office until his death in 1972.)

1917: During World War I, the French execute the exotic dancer Mata Hari (born Margaretha Geertruida Zelle), claiming she is a German spy. Her conviction was based on a secret court martial and little evidence.

- **1930s:** Five students at England's Cambridge University— later known as the Cambridge Five—are recruited to spy for the Soviet Union. Their espionage continues for three decades and proves devastating to Great Britain and America.

- **1940:** The FBI deploys more than 350 special agents in Latin America in the hunt for German spies. This is done under a unit named the Special Intelligence Service (SIS), which is disbanded at the end of World War II. The Bureau also actively searches for German and Japanese spies in America.

- **1942:** The Office of Strategic Services (OSS) is created in the United States during World War II. The OSS is founded as an intelligence and covert-action agency under the famous General "Wild Bill" Donovan. It, too, is disbanded at the end of World War II and is later succeeded by the Central Intelligence Agency (CIA).

- **1947:** President Harry S. Truman signs the National Security Act, creating the National Security Council and the CIA, the beginnings of today's intelligence community.

- **1953:** Julius and Ethel Rosenberg are executed in the United States for espionage on behalf of the Soviet Union (also called the USSR). The Rosenbergs were members of an atomic spy ring whose espionage helped the USSR develop its own nuclear bomb.

• **1959:** The United States successfully launches the CORONA spy satellite, after twelve unsuccessful attempts. The satellite takes images of the USSR from space. The spy satellite program is a big breakthrough for the United States in the Cold War.

• **1960:** An American pilot, Lieutenant Francis Gary Powers, is shot down over the USSR while flying a U-2 spy plane. He is captured, tried, and convicted of espionage. Later he is exchanged for Soviet intelligence colonel Rudolf Abel, who was imprisoned in the United States for his espionage activities.

• **1994:** Aldrich Ames is arrested for selling U.S. secrets to the Soviets, beginning in 1985 when he was head of a CIA Soviet counterintelligence unit. His betrayal led to the executions of at least ten Soviet intelligence officers who had been secretly cooperating with the CIA and FBI.

• **2001:** Robert Hanssen, a twenty-five-year FBI veteran, is arrested for passing U.S. secrets to Russia. His betrayal was more damaging than Ames's. He revealed how the

United States was gathering intelligence from Russia, which resulted in the loss of some very expensive technical operations. (See "The Cost of Betrayal," page 16.)

- **September 11, 2001:** Nineteen Arab terrorists hijack four commercial aircraft in the United States and fly two into New York City's World Trade Center and one into the Pentagon in Virginia; the fourth plane crashes in a field in Pennsylvania. All told, roughly 3,000 people are killed. This incident, which follows other terrorist attacks, leads President George W. Bush to declare a "war on terror" against Islamic extremists, notably Al Qaeda. Al Qaeda is led by former Saudi businessman Osama Bin Laden, who earlier declared war on America.

- **2002:** Former U.S. Defense Intelligence Agency (DIA) analyst Ana Montes is sentenced to twenty-five years in prison for espionage on behalf of Cuba.

- **2006:** Alexander Litvinenko, a defector from Russian intelligence, dies of radiation poisoning in London. On his deathbed, Litvinenko accuses Russian president Vladimir Putin of masterminding his assassination.

- **2008:** Chi Mak, a naturalized U.S. citizen, is sentenced to twenty-four and a half years in prison for espionage on behalf of China. An engineer working for a defense contracting company, Mak had been stealing sensitive defense technology for several years and relaying it to Beijing.

The Cost of Betrayal

When an American intelligence officer is arrested for giving secrets to another country, a public affidavit detailing the charges is issued. These affidavits, which are sworn statements of fact, can be quite revealing.

For example, Ronald Pelton, a former National Security Agency (NSA) intelligence officer, sold secrets to the Soviet Union in the early 1980s. The affidavit accused him of informing the Soviets that the Americans were running submarines up the Russian coast to wiretap undersea cables. Those wiretaps let the Americans listen to Soviet military communications and track Soviet submarines. The operation, which cost two to three billion dollars, had to be abandoned after that. After his arrest, Pelton was heard to say that the Soviets paid him about $35,000 for the secrets.

In another example, FBI Special Agent Robert Hanssen let the Russians know that the United States had built a tunnel underneath the Russian embassy in Washington, D.C. The tunnel would have allowed the Americans to listen in on the Russians' conversations. Once again, a very expensive operation had to be abandoned.

From the Soviet Union to Russia

The Soviet Union, or the USSR, was formed in 1922. During World War II, the Soviets and Americans fought on the same side.

After the war, however, the United States and the Soviet Union emerged as the world's two superpowers. The United States opposed Soviet military expansion and its support of international communism. The conflict was known as the Cold War because they didn't fight on the battlefield. Instead, each country employed thousands of spies who did their best to gather information on their opponents. The Soviet Union's main intelligence and security agency was known as the Committee for State Security (KGB).

In 1991, the Soviet Union broke up into fifteen independent republics. Russia is the most powerful of those new countries.

WHY DO WE NEED SPIES?

Every country wants to know what other countries—both friends and enemies—are doing and how it might affect their national interests. Countries also spy on groups of people, such as terrorists, who may not work for a foreign government but who pose great threats to national security and safety.

All the information collected and analyzed is called intelligence, which is why organizations like the CIA are called intelligence agencies. The information can be gathered in many ways. One method (and the basis of many spy novels and movies) is by recruiting people who will give the agencies information. These people are called sources, agents, or assets. The information they give is called human intelligence, or HUMINT.

Another intelligence-gathering method relies on technical gadgetry rather than people. Information that's gathered by using satellites and aircraft is called imagery intelligence, or IMINT. Information discovered by electronic means, such as intercepting conversations or Internet traffic, is called signals intelligence, or SIGINT.

SPY SPEAK

HUMINT:

An acronym that stands for "human intelligence," or information that's been obtained through people.

IMINT:

An acronym that stands for "imagery intelligence," or photos that have been gathered by satellites and aircraft.

SIGINT:

An acronym that stands for "signals intelligence," or information that's been collected electronically.

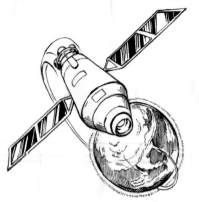

OSINT:

An acronym that stands for "open-source intelligence," or information that's been obtained from sources available to the public.

WHO GETS TO BE CALLED A SPY?

The term "spy" is used very loosely and can refer to anyone who gathers secret information, whether for the government or not. However, in the intelligence community the term is used more precisely. Here's a quick breakdown:

Anyone who works in intelligence is known as an intelligence officer (sometimes called an I.O. for short).

Most intelligence officers are analysts. They go through all the intelligence that comes in from the field and analyze that raw information to try to figure out what's happening around the world and what could happen in the future.

The intelligence officers who work around the world are often called case officers. They are the ones who actually conduct espionage and operate as spies. Unlike James Bond and other movie spies, they almost never have to sneak into highly guarded buildings to steal secrets, though sometimes they do.

Instead, they usually find people who have access to the information they want. They recruit those people as agents. The case officer manages, or "runs," these sources by letting them know what kind of information they need. Usually, intelligence officers think of the sources they recruit in the field as the real spies.

To help you keep everything straight, here's a little chart:

Intelligence Officer	What He/She Does:
Case Officer (a.k.a. operations officer)	Recruits agents (a.k.a. sources or assets), who gather intelligence.
Analyst	Analyzes intelligence from the field.

Intelligence officers do different jobs, but they can all be called spies!

SPY SPEAK

a.k.a.:

An acronym meaning "also known as." For example, the infamous terrorist Ilich Ramírez Sánchez was often called "Carlos the Jackal," so he might be referred to as Ilich Ramírez Sánchez, a.k.a. Carlos the Jackal.

Agent:

A person who has been recruited to get secret information and give it to an intelligence officer. Also known as a source or asset.

An intelligence officer tries to get information that will:

- protect our country from threats
- figure out what other countries' spies are doing against our country—this is called counterintelligence.

SPY SPEAK

Intelligence:

Information and analysis about another country's or organization's secrets.

Intelligence officer:

Any person who works for an intelligence agency in collection or analysis.

Counterintelligence:

Activities that combat—or protect a country from—foreign threats, such as espionage, sabotage, and terrorism. These are usually conducted by counterintelligence officers.

During a time of war or political crisis, a spy might be told to get the answers to these kinds of questions:

- What are other countries' military strengths and weaknesses?
- Are they building more weapons, warplanes, and tanks?
- Are they planning to attack another country, or are they expecting an attack?
- Is there a civil war brewing?
- What could happen internationally if civil war breaks out?
- What could happen if there's a coup and the leadership is overthrown?

 SPY SPEAK

Civil war:

A war between two opposing groups within one country.

Coup:

A sudden overthrow of a government, followed by a seizure of power. (Pronounced "coo"; from the French word *coup*, meaning "a sharp blow.")

It may seem as if spies are only interested in military secrets. And it's true that military and terrorist attacks are two of the most dramatic threats any country can face. But spies want to know everything about the world—after all, it's sometimes hard to tell what kind of secrets will end up being important. So they may also try to find out what kinds of trade agreements or treaties are being developed between two countries.

Technology is another major focus of spying. You'll often

read about spies being caught in California's Silicon Valley, one of the centers of the computer industry, or in Los Alamos, New Mexico, where the atomic bomb was developed and scientific research continues today. If another country can steal the secret of a new technology, it can save billions of dollars and years of work that would be needed to develop that technology from scratch. But when the spying is done by a business competitor, rather than by a foreign country, it is called corporate espionage.

For example, during World War II, the Soviet Union and the United States were allies—they fought on the same side. However, at the same time Soviet spies stole the secret of the atomic bomb, which had been developed by the United States. That helped the Soviet Union create its own atomic bomb about two years before it could have developed it on its own.

Whether spies are getting information on terror plots or new technology, the goal is to figure out what's happening in the world—not the world as we'd like it to be, but the world as it *really* is.

SPY SPEAK

Corporate espionage:
Spying by one private company on another solely to gain a business advantage. The spying company, which may be foreign or one in our own country, is not trying to learn national security secrets to pass to its own government, but commercial secrets.

CHAPTER 2

WHAT IS A SPY?

et's be honest: Not everyone wants to dodge bullets or face down danger as a spy. (Some of us get nervous just thinking about it.) The good news? There are all types of jobs within the sixteen government agencies that make up the U.S. intelligence community. (See appendix A, on page 139.) Those jobs are roughly divided into two groups with two different missions: learning (intelligence gathering) and understanding (intelligence analysis).

Most spies don't get to drive a supercool car or fight evil villains the way James Bond does. However, in many ways, their work is even more interesting, because it's real.

What Spies Don't Do

Many people are confused about the difference between a detective and a spy. Simply put, a detective solves crimes, either as a member of a police department or as a private operative. Spies, on the other hand, don't bring criminals to justice—their responsibility is getting information to help the American government make foreign policy and national security decisions.

SO WHAT KIND OF WORK COULD I DO?

That depends on which government agency you join. For example, the CIA collects information that relates to U.S. national security and foreign policy. For that reason, the CIA works mainly in countries other than the United States.

The FBI deals mostly with law enforcement within the United States. In today's world, that also includes gathering intelligence on terrorist groups.

The NSA deals with the breaking of foreign codes and the interception of electronically transmitted information, such as phone calls and e-mails.

Other agencies, such as the State Department (which sets and maintains foreign policy) and the Treasury Department (which collects taxes and maintains federal finances) also have intelligence branches. However, they are usually much smaller and deal mostly with analysis. In addition to these branches, each of the military services has an intelligence group as well.

When people think of spies, however, they tend to think of the CIA, otherwise known simply as the Agency (sometimes referred to as the Company). Let's take a closer look at the CIA.

The CIA is divided into four branches. Each branch hires intelligence officers to do different types of work. The four branches are:

The National Clandestine Service (NCS)

The NCS staff includes operations officers, also known as case officers. They work mainly overseas at field posts called stations. During the Cold War, a CIA station could also be connected with an official American organization.

The case officers recruit local people to get them secret information. These local people are called agents, sources, or assets.

You Say Po-tay-to, I Say Po-tah-to

Want to sound like a real insider at the CIA or the FBI? Then you'd better make sure you can talk the talk! Try taking this little quiz:

What does the CIA call the people who give them information?
Agents, sources, or assets.
What does the FBI call those same people?
Informants.

In the same way the CIA uses the terms "case officer" and "operations officer" for the people who recruit sources, the FBI calls their staff officers "special agents."

You don't need to worry too much about all these different terms until you get your job as a spy—and then you'll simply use the same label as everyone else in your agency, whether you're with the CIA or the FBI.

The Directorate of Intelligence (DI)

Staff officers in the DI are called analysts. These officers pore over raw intelligence, including information sent back by case officers, photos from spy satellites, news picked up from foreign media, and much more. Then they analyze the material to determine what it all means. Finally, they create formal reports, which are sent to selected government officials, starting with the president of the United States and his chief national security advisers.

When these reports are sent out, they're said to have been published, distributed, or disseminated. When they deal with major issues, they're sometimes called national intelligence estimates, which means they are based on information from other agencies in the intelligence community, not just the CIA. When the agencies disagree on certain points, the reports include footnotes so that the reader understands what the differences of opinion are.

SPY SPEAK

National Intelligence Estimate (NIE):

A long-term or strategic report on a major topic that includes input from all other intelligence agencies.

The Directorate of Science and Technology (DS&T)

The DS&T includes engineers, technicians, scientists, crafts-men, artists, and social scientists. They design a wide range of intelligence-gathering and analytical tools, including satellite programs, computer technology, and the various gadgets, or technical devices, used by case officers in the field. DS&T officers also travel abroad to operate their gadgets or assist local NCS officers in using them.

The Directorate of Administration (DA)

This directorate handles all the day-to-day workings of the huge government organization that is the CIA. Yes, even the CIA has people in charge of hiring employees, providing medical support, writing contracts, and fixing employees' computers!

WHAT ARE SOME MYTHS ABOUT SPYING?

Many people secretly dream of becoming spies. They all have different reasons, but here are some of the most common:

- They crave excitement and adventure.
- They're motivated by patriotism and a desire to serve their country.

- They're very curious about the world and interested in learning more about it.

However, most people's idea of what a spy's life is like comes from novels and movies. Before getting into the nitty-gritty of how to apply for a job in intelligence, let's take a look at a few common myths about spying—and the realities.

MYTH: **You're in constant danger**

REALITY: There *is* an element of danger when you're a spy—there's no doubt about that. But a lot of intelligence officers work at desk jobs in the United States. And even the case officers who work overseas are often stationed there in some sort of official cover capacity that doesn't keep them 100% safe.

"Official cover" means they are connected with an official American organization. This gives them some protection, since they are government officials.

However, some intelligence officers live in foreign countries undercover as private individuals doing everyday kinds of jobs. They're said to be working under nonofficial cover (NOC), which means they don't have official protection.

Often the biggest threat to an intelligence officer is that his true status as a spy will be exposed. When that happens, he has been "burned." The local government declares him persona non grata, or PNG, which is the diplomatic way a government says he is no longer welcome in a country. In fact, the local government may even throw the officer out of the country.

Most novels, movies, and TV shows about spies depict them in constant—and deadly—danger. In real life, the odds are fairly good that you won't end up facing someone with a gun in a dark alley.

Having said that, it's also true that today more spies are involved in fighting international terrorism, which has led to more intelligence officers carrying weapons and finding themselves in life-threatening situations. For example, CIA officer Johnny Michael Spann was the first American killed when the United States invaded Afghanistan in 2001.

 # SPY SPEAK

Burned:

What an intelligence officer is said to be when his cover and work as a spy are exposed.

Persona non grata (PNG):

Latin for "unwelcome person." Anyone declared persona non grata when working in a foreign country usually has to leave.

Official cover:

What an intelligence officer is said to have when working for an organization officially affiliated with his or her own government.

Nonofficial cover (NOC):

What an intelligence officer is said to have when working in a foreign country undercover as a private individual, without any official status as an employee of his or her government.

MYTH: You have to kill people

REALITY: Most people who work for an intelligence agency never have to fire a gun, let alone kill someone. The spying game is more about learning secrets in sneaky ways than having shootouts. Real spy weapons, like the lipstick pistol or umbrella gun, are the exception, not the rule.

MYTH: You lead a glamorous and exciting life

REALITY: Living and working overseas does tend to be more exciting and fast paced than staying at home. But remember: You not only have to get your office work done—which may include having to perform a cover job—you also have to make time to recruit and run your agents!

MYTH: You get to travel the world

REALITY: Well, actually, this *is* true. Certainly if you're a case officer, you'll probably be assigned to live and work in foreign countries. This is becoming true for analysts as well. Intelligence agencies are trying to send their analysts into the field so that they can develop greater expertise and gain first-hand knowledge of the area they're focusing on. Analysts may work overseas for six months to a year.

Many officers specialize in specific geographic areas, such as the Middle East, Africa, or Europe. So if you're assigned to Egypt, you'll live and work in Egypt, but you may carry out cover assignments in other countries. You won't travel all over the world. (Of course, Egypt is pretty cool, so who cares if you don't get to go to Monte Carlo or Moscow?)

MYTH: **You're applauded for being a spy, and everyone thinks you're really cool!**

REALITY: This is absolutely not true! In fact, if you want to be in the spotlight, you should not go into the spying business.

First of all, no one gets credit for something that *doesn't* happen. Let's say that you, as a spy, manage to thwart a major terrorist attack on Americans. Great! But the public will never know about that because spy agencies are— what a surprise!—really secretive.

So if you want to take a bow and hear applause, maybe you should become an actor instead of a spy . . .

SPY QUIZ

Do You Have the Right Spy Stuff?

1) **You've been invited to a formal wedding. You wear:**
   a) A nice dress (if you're a girl) or pants, a jacket, and a tie (if you're a boy)—the wedding *is* formal, after all.
   b) Jeans and a T-shirt—hey, you want to be comfortable!
   c) An outrageous party outfit—you want to have fun at the reception.

2) **You have a ticket to see a movie downtown, but you just found out the bus you were going to take has a flat tire and you don't have time to wait for the next bus. You:**
   a) Throw a tantrum, right there in the bus line, screaming and shouting that your life has been ruined.
   b) Start calling friends on your cell phone to see if they can give you a lift, while looking at the bus map to see if you can walk a few blocks to catch another bus.
   c) Sigh and decide that you just won't get to see that movie after all. Oh, well. Life is unfair.

3) Every day, you ride the bus to school. The bus always takes the same route. If someone asked you to describe your daily ride, you would:

a) Stare at them blankly. You spend your bus ride daydreaming or chatting with friends.

b) Describe in detail every house and business you pass, including how many dogs are in each yard, which store has just put up a GOING OUT OF BUSINESS sign, and which driveways always have at least one car in them when you go past.

c) Talk about some major landmarks, but that's about it.

4) When a friend tells you a secret, you:

a) Never tell another person (unless, of course, keeping the secret would put your friend in harm's way).

b) Spill the beans within twenty-four hours. You're just a natural gossip.

c) Never tell another person, period.

5) You've been invited to a dinner party that begins at 6 P.M. You:

a) Arrive twenty minutes early—hey, it never hurts to get there first.

b) Arrive ten minutes late—you missed the bus and had to walk.

c) Arrive at 6 P.M. sharp—you're always right on time.

Answers

1) If you checked *a*, you'd make a good spy. Spies try to blend into their surroundings and look like they belong at all times. If you checked *b* or *c*, you would stand out—possibly a good distraction, but not good If you're undercover.

2) If you checked *b*, you have the makings of a good intelligence officer. When the unexpected happens, you immediately start figuring out what to do next. Even better, you explore a couple of different options. If you checked *a*, you have some work to do! Making a scene will draw attention—and that's the last thing a spy wants. If you checked *c*, you probably give up too easily to be a spy.

3) A spy-in-training would definitely check *b*! Most people don't pay any attention to their surroundings. If you asked them where you could get a shoe heel fixed, they'd have no idea, because they never notice the shoe repair shop around the corner. A spy is always alert and watchful. So use that boring bus ride to practice your observation skills!

4) You might think the right answer is *c*. After all, spies are supposed to be tight-lipped, right? But actually, *a* is the better answer. That's because spies also have to use good judgment and common sense. If your friend told you that he was planning to do something dangerous, it would be better to let an adult or someone responsible know.

5) If you checked *c*, you would make a good spy—spies tend to have an excellent sense of time. They know exactly how long it takes to travel to their destination, and they plan to arrive at exactly the appointed time.

◎◎ Spy Story

In 1985, Oleg Gordievsky was working as a Soviet spy in London. His cover story was that he was a diplomat. He was doing very well as an intelligence officer—in fact, he was in line to become the KGB's resident, or chief spy, in England. But then his bosses ordered him back to Moscow.

The KGB suspected that he was working for the British. And they were right! Gordievsky knew he would be in serious danger if they discovered the truth and would probably be killed. Recalled to Moscow, he was given a truth serum drug and interrogated about his activities. Although Gordievsky managed to maintain his innocence and was released, he knew he had to escape from the Soviet Union.

He contacted MI6, the British intelligence agency, and asked for help. He was told to go to a certain lamppost in Moscow at 7 P.M., carrying a grocery store bag to identify himself. If the signal was received, a man eating a candy bar and carrying a grocery bag from the famous London store Harrods would stroll by.

After almost a half-hour wait, a man carrying a Harrods

bag made eye contact with Gordievsky. The operation had begun.

For the next few days, Gordievsky would duck into buildings as he walked around town, to see if anyone was following. Sure enough, he spotted KGB agents on his trail. However, he managed to buy a train ticket for the Russian-Finnish border without alerting them to his plans.

When he got to the border, he was met by British intelligence officers, who smuggled him out in the trunk of their car. And, in a twist worthy of James Bond, the British intelligence officers provided Gordievsky with a thermal blanket. Why? Because the heat given off by the blanket would interfere with Soviet scanning equipment so that the border control would not be able to tell he was in the car. This simple maneuver allowed Gordievsky to escape across the border—to freedom.

WHAT DO SPIES DO?

How do spies know what to look for—what secrets to steal, what offices to bug, which people to follow? Like anyone else with a job to do, they focus first on the assignment their bosses give them. They get those assignments as part of the intelligence cycle.

The intelligence cycle starts with the Top Boss, or, as he or she is otherwise known, the president of the United States. The president and the people who work with him are called policy makers. They want accurate and timely information about what's going on in the world because that helps them decide how the United States should deal with its friends and its enemies.

Here's how the intelligence cycle works:

1

The policy makers tell the intelligence agencies what kind of information they need. For example, they may want more details about the relationship between Iran and Iraq, or they may need a closer look at a civil war brewing in Africa.

2

The intelligence agencies figure out how to get this information and then direct their intelligence officers to collect it. However, the intelligence officers don't just give their bosses what they've been asked for. They must stay alert and report any threats or important information that the policy makers clearly need to know.

This step is the basis of every spy movie ever filmed! The information is gathered in one of three ways:

- from case officers and the agents they've recruited
- from technological gizmos like wiretaps, bugs, and spy satellites
- from sources available to any member of the public, such as the news media or government reports.

3

6

Step Six: The reports are sent to top government officials, such as the secretary of state. Once the officials have read the reports, they often have other questions. Those questions are sent to the intelligence agencies, which then develop a plan to answer them . . . and the whole cycle starts again! It's a continuous loop that never ends.

Step Five: Analysts study the processed information and figure out what it all means. They then write detailed reports on the findings. These reports—which may be given as a written document, a graphic, or an oral presentation—are called "intelligence product."

5

PDB

For example, every day the president is given a blue binder with a report from the director of national intelligence (DNI). It's called the President's Daily Brief (PDB). The PDB reports on and analyzes burning issues of national security importance—kind of like the newspaper, only much scarier!

Step Four: This step is often called "processing and exploitation." This simply means that someone must take raw data and turn it into something that can be studied. For example,

4

the transcript of a conversation in a foreign language must be translated, coded messages have to be deciphered, some information may need to be prepared for computer processing, and so on.

SPY SPEAK

Bug:

A miniature listening device used to secretly eavesdrop on and probably transmit a person's private conversations.

President's Daily Brief (PDB):

A report prepared by U.S. intelligence agencies for the president that informs him on critical issues of national security importance.

WHAT ARE A SPY'S MAIN RESPONSIBILITIES?

Discover the ground truth

In the military, the phrase "ground truth" means the reality of a situation; that is, what's *really* happening, rather than what people behind the front lines or at home *wish* was happening.

In the intelligence community, the goal is always to discover the ground truth and then to pass it on through the intelligence cycle. So how does a spy do that?

Think of an intelligence officer as a very good investigative reporter. Reporters try to get people to talk to them in confidence. They try to get people to identify other people who may have key bits of information. They try to get photos or other physical or electronic evidence to support the information in their reporting.

Spies do all that, too. The difference is that they are working for their government, not for a newspaper or magazine. But both spies and reporters want to find out the truth. They want to get the facts.

During the long history of spying, spies raced to get information back to their military commanders or the rulers in their home countries. Today, spy satellites can instantly send photos of events from around the world, and even the average citizen can watch CNN's around-the-clock coverage. For example, in 1989 everyone could watch the

protests in China's Tiananmen Square and people tearing down the Berlin Wall *as the events were unfolding*.

However, it's still critically important to know what *caused* those events, how other countries' leaders and governments are reacting, and how they plan to respond, now and in the future.

Of course, it's almost impossible to predict exactly what will happen, although intelligence agencies do their best to figure out when something like a terrorist attack is going to take place. However, it *is* possible to try to understand the nature of the threats facing one's country and how they are growing or changing. A spy seeks to understand what unfriendly nations and organizations are capable of doing, what their plans or intentions are, and how to expose or prevent hostile actions against his or her own country.

Finally, intelligence officers do more than just report on what they've been directed to look at. They also have to look ahead and try to figure out what trouble is brewing on the horizon. For example, perhaps you've been assigned to follow what's happening in Zimbabwe. Maybe no one has asked you about what's going on in South Africa. But because you've got your eyes and ears open, you've noticed something that leads you to say, "In addition to what's happening in Zimbabwe, it looks as if South Africa is planning an invasion." Your bosses may not have thought to ask you about this, but it's your job to try to see into the future—at least a little.

Stop the other guys

Spies are also often involved in counterintelligence. That means working to stop another country's spies from doing *their* job—which is stealing secrets from the United States.

It's a bit like that old *MAD* magazine comic strip called *Spy vs. Spy*. The comic featured two cartoon characters, one dressed in black and one dressed in white. In every strip, each one would try to foil the other's attempts to set booby traps.

In the real world, of course, counterintelligence is quite a bit more serious. Other countries often spy on the United States in order to steal new technologies that have been developed by scientists and private companies. This may not seem as important as getting information about a country's military forces or nuclear weapons, but it's actually very significant. The reason is simple: If other countries can get this kind of information, they don't have to figure out how to build new technologies on their own. That can save them billions of dollars and many years of work.

Conduct covert actions

Finally, intelligence officers are sometimes ordered to take action to influence events. These actions are called covert, which simply means secret. A covert action (CA) is carried out in such a way that—in theory, at least—no one knows who did it. (This often requires "plausible denial," which means that your government can claim that it wasn't involved.)

In real life, however, covert actions often become public knowledge. Sometimes a presidential administration is proud of the action it has taken and leaks details to the press. That was the case when the United States helped the mujahideen drive the Soviets from Afghanistan in the 1980s. In other cases, the covert action goes so wrong that the public ends up finding out about it.

Covert actions can include planting newspaper articles, secretly giving money to opposition groups, or overthrowing another government or getting someone else to do it.

Executive Order 12333 prohibits U.S. intelligence agencies from carrying out assassinations or hiring other people to do so. However, in the midst of a war, enemy leaders are considered legitimate targets. That's why you sometimes read about missiles targeting high-level terrorist leaders. (This is called targeted killing, rather than assassination.)

Major covert actions must be directed by a signed order by the president, which is called a presidential finding. This sort of order is usually classified, which means that it's an official secret that is only known to authorized people.

SPY SPEAK

Classified:

Officially secret and accessible only to people with a need to know.

Need to know:

The restriction of sensitive data to government officials cleared to know about a certain case or operation.

Your Spy Competition

American spies pit their brains and cunning against spies from other countries. Here are a few of the top players you'll be going up against if you become a spy:

Russia

The SVR, or Sluzhba Vneshney Razvedk

During the Cold War, the United States faced off against the Soviet Union and that country's fabled spy agency, the KGB. After the Soviet Union broke up, Russia created the SVR to take the place of the KGB. Many believe that Russia's spying within the United States is now back to Cold War levels.

China

The MSS, or Ministry of State Security

The Chinese use a different method of spying than Western countries. Instead of using only a few agents to find out secret information, the MSS will use many cooperating sources to try to get a fact, no matter how small. The

Chinese will then put all those facts together to find out, for example, how a U.S. weapons system is made. The MSS focuses on high-tech industries and military technology.

India

RAW, or Research and Analysis Wing

RAW was founded in 1968 to counter Pakistani militant groups in India. Over the years, the agency has become involved in activities in other countries. In addition to Pakistan, RAW focuses on Sri Lanka, Nepal, and Bangladesh.

Pakistan

The ISI, or Inter-Services Intelligence

The ISI worked with the United States to drive the Soviet occupiers out of Afghanistan in the 1980s and later to fight against antigovernment terrorists in Pakistan. However, India has accused the ISI of being involved in dozens of terrorist attacks launched in Pakistan against Indian interests.

Great Britain

MI6

This agency is familiar to any James Bond fan! Founded in 1909 to spy on Germany, the agency came into its own during the Cold War, dueling with Moscow's KGB. Like other Western intelligence services, MI6 initially reacted sluggishly to the emergence of post—Cold War threats, such as terrorism, but has caught up to modern times—it now recruits by advertising in newspapers and even in spy-themed computer games found online!

WHAT DO SPIES DO?

Israel

The Mossad

The Mossad, which means "the Institute," was founded in 1951. Most spies, no matter who they work for, regard this agency as one of the most skilled and aggressive in the world. It excels not only at gathering intelligence on its Arab neighbors but also at selectively assassinating terrorists deemed a threat to Israel.

IN WHICH AREA OF INTELLIGENCE SHOULD I CONSIDER WORKING?

That depends a lot on your personality and interests! If you're social and outgoing, you might do quite well in gathering intelligence. If you love to hit the books and solve puzzles, a job as an analyst could be right for you. And if you enjoy taking apart alarm clocks and inventing new gizmos, you probably belong in the science and technology department.

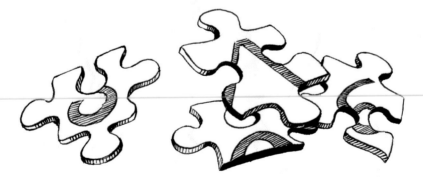

Operations

Case officers (also known as operations officers) come the closest to doing the job that most people imagine when they think of spies. They often have a real job overseas, which is called their cover. It's the official reason that they're living and working in that foreign country.

During the day, they have to do that job. But when they're off duty, they're trying to develop, recruit, and run sources.

You've probably noticed that having an official cover also has a downside—namely, you have to work two jobs. So you might sit at your desk during the day, writing reports about the country's economic conditions. Then you might go meet agents at night or on the weekends as part of your job for the CIA.

So let's say you're a case officer working in a foreign country. You've got your day job, but what are your duties when it comes to actually *spying*?

You don't usually have to break into offices at midnight and steal microfilm. Instead, you have to recruit sources, local people who can give you inside information. Once a case officer has won her source's trust, she meets with that person on a regular basis. This is called running an agent.

How does recruitment work?

First, you have to figure out what your target is. What kind of information are you trying to get? Maybe you're trying to find out what's going on in the government, in the political parties, in the military, or in the labor unions of the country that you've been assigned to.

Once you know what kind of information you want, you think of ways to get access to people who could give you the information. For example, if you're interested in what's going on with labor unions, you might go to a meeting and see if you could strike up a conversation with someone there. Or maybe you read about someone in the newspaper and realize that person would be a good source who could help you. You would try to meet him in some natural way and not tell him who you are.

It's a lot like networking in order to get a job. If you want a job at a certain company, you rack your brain to think of anyone you know who works in that field and who might have a contact for you. When you get a contact, you try to meet that person and see if he can give you information about available jobs, other people to call, and so forth.

As a spy, you may run into someone playing tennis and strike up a conversation. The meeting seems accidental, but of course, you actually targeted that person because you thought he could get you information. Then you did some research and found out he was an avid tennis player. After that, you figured out a way to join his country club or sign up for a tennis tournament so you could meet him.

Once you've been introduced, you do your best to be friendly and charming—someone he wants to talk to again. You start to develop the relationship—playing more games of tennis, going to lunch, maybe finding other areas of mutual interest.

And all the time you're doing this, you're trying to figure out if he can help you get the secrets you want. This is a critical part of a spy's job: assessing the possible agent. First, you have to determine if the person has access to what you want. Second, you have to get a sense of how willing he might be to work secretly for the U.S. government. After all, being a spy could endanger his reputation, his job and, in some countries, even his life.

It can take months or years to develop the relationship and to find out if the person you're befriending is a good risk. You will spend hours and hours chatting with this person. And all the time, you're probing to see what kind of person he really is. It's as if you're a talented salesperson who is trying to spot openings that will help you sell something to a customer.

Once you've floated the idea that he might help you get some information and he's agreed, then you're in the relationship for the long haul. You have to build trust with your agents, because they're entrusting you with their lives. You end up knowing more about them than their own spouses because they're confiding in you about their lives, their problems, what's going on with their kids, everything! Of course, sometimes you get tired of listening to your agents, especially if they're always complaining, but you weigh that against the value of the information you're getting.

Not only can recruitment take a lot of time, but also it doesn't always work! In fact, there are probably more failures than successes. So you must have a lot of patience and determination.

How does a case officer learn to do all this?

Once you're hired by the CIA, you'll get about six months of training at the Farm, a large training site in Virginia. (See chapter 5 for more details on the training.)

Does all that training make you a great spy?

Well, it helps. But it still takes one or two tours of duty to figure out what you're doing, whether you're any good at it, and whether you want to do it. (A tour is a two-to-three-year stint.) So if you get this far, be patient and learn everything you can! Being a spy is a complicated job that takes time to learn, but it's always interesting.

SPY SPEAK

Tour:

A set amount of time (generally two to three years) that an intelligence officer spends in a given assignment.

What kinds of people make good case officers?

Some highly successful case officers are naturals, like athletes who have an inborn gift for their sport. (Even naturals, however, benefit from coaching and formal training.) If you're outgoing and can talk easily to people, you have the right personality for the job. Case officers are often those people who always want parties to last a little longer. If people are starting to go home, the case officer is the one who says, "Hey, let's all go out dancing!"

SPY'S GUIDE TO BEING A SPY

ROLL	SCENE	TAKE
3	1	1

But even if you're not always the life of the party, you might still do well in this field. A case officer is also, in a sense, an actor. After all, when you're recruiting someone, you're actually playing a part. Your role is that of an engaging person who wants to strike up a friendship. Like many real actors, you might be rather shy. Even shy actors, however, have a great time once the camera rolls or they step onstage, because they get to pretend to be someone else.

Does a case officer tell his kids about what he does or does he lie to them?

That depends on how old the kids are and how well they can keep a secret. Younger children often repeat things—in perfect innocence—that their parents would rather keep private. Obviously, a spy doesn't want his five-year-old to blow his cover! But once children get to be a little older, a parent could certainly confide in them about the secret nature of his job.

INTELLIGENCE AND ANALYSIS

Intelligence officers who work with information or analyze it are called analysts. Thousands of analysts work in the intelligence community—in fact, there are many more analysts than case officers. (Former CIA director George Tenet once said at a congressional hearing that there are more FBI special agents working in New York City than there are CIA case officers around the world!) The analyst sifts through all the intelligence that's been collected and figures out what it all means.

This is a huge job. Think about all the different ways that intelligence is collected. We get it from spy satellites, human agents, electronic communications intercepts, and open-sourcc information.

Open-source information is everything that's available to the public through media or declassified documents. For example, an analyst who's assigned to France will read French newspapers, listen to French radio, and watch French TV. After all, why go to the trouble of recruiting an agent and paying her to give you information when you can get it by reading it online?

In the last decade or so, there's been an explosion of open-source information that once would have cost millions of dollars to obtain. Today, interested citizens can access much of that intelligence on their own. For example, you can go to Google Earth and get an overhead satellite photo of Moscow or Beijing.

An analyst has to look for the important facts among all the data, make sense of them, and then draw conclusions about what's happening now and what might happen in the future. This job is like sifting for gold: An analyst tries to pick out the nuggets that are useful and have meaning. The analyst then writes a finished intelligence report, which goes to the person in the government who makes policy, such as the president or the secretary of state.

The president and his advisers and other policy makers will then ask questions about the report and ask for more information. For example, perhaps the analyst has written that there's a plot to assassinate a certain world leader. The president may ask, "Well, if that plot succeeds, who will be put in place to run the country? Tell me who you think will take power." Those questions go back to the analyst, who sifts through all the information to find the answers and then writes another report.

TMI!

It's better to have too much intelligence than too little, but this can lead to a new problem. Trying to sort through so much information can be like trying to take a drink of water from a fire hose. An analyst has to sift through thousands of unimportant facts to find the few that are significant.

Then she has to figure out what those facts mean. She can tell what's happening now . . . but what's going to happen next?

The frustrating thing is that you can't predict the future with any certainty. For example, former CIA director George Tenet warned people before 9/11 that some kind of terrorist action was going to occur—but he didn't know when the attack would happen or that it would involve hijacked planes being flown into the World Trade Center.

An analyst could have pointed out that Al Qaeda had attacked the World Trade Center in 1993 but did not succeed in knocking down the towers. The analyst might have added that Al Qaeda has a history of finishing jobs they start. Finally, the analyst could have noted a CIA report that said terrorists might use aircraft as part of their attack. That still would not have given the crucial bits of information—time, date, and method—necessary to prevent the 9/11 attacks. However, it might have alerted other government authorities, such as those overseeing the airlines, to notify the airlines to take extra precautions. If that had been done, the 9/11 attacks might have been prevented.

 SPY SPEAK

Open-source information (OSINT):

Everything that's available to the public, such as newspapers, magazines, TV, and radio shows, scientific journals, Web sites, and declassified or unclassified government documents.

Eyes only:

A security restriction on documents that lets you know that you can read the material but should not discuss it with anyone else who is not cleared for that case. "Cleared" simply means that someone has permission or access to information on a particular case or situation.

Intelligence in an Age of Terror

U.S. intelligence has played a leading role in the "war on terror," which was declared by President Bush following the 9/11 attacks. The development of unmanned, low-flying drones (Unmanned Aerial Vehicles, or UAVs) is one of the latest intelligence-gathering techniques used in countering the terrorists. Armed drones have also been used to attack terrorist strongholds and kill terrorist leaders. The terrorists also rely heavily on their own intelligence capabilities and covert tradecraft to plan and carry out their deadly activities.

What kinds of people make good analysts?

There are certain personality types that seem to gravitate toward analysis. Typically, they're detail-oriented, love to read and discover, and are dogged researchers—analysts often burn the midnight oil to get their reports just right.

SCIENCE AND TECHNOLOGY

If you're interested in science, computers, or gadgets, you could aim for a career on the technology side of spying. After all, someone has to come up with new overhead reconnaissance satellites and design those wristwatch cameras and invisible inks!

Seriously, intelligence agencies do hire people to come up with gadgets that sound like something from a spy movie. In addition, computer scientists and programmers work on creating and breaking codes or intercepting e-mails or cell phone calls.

Those expensive spy satellites that can take a photo from outer space need to be designed and maintained, too.

Of course, intelligence agencies also need people who are fluent in foreign languages, understand economics, have studied other cultures, and know a bit about psychology.

DS&T includes:

- Covert communications, or COVCOM, which includes techniques to develop ways for case officers and agents to talk or leave messages in secret. This group works on secret writing, short-range radio, subminiature cameras, special film, high-frequency broadcasts, satellite communications, and microdots (a microscopic printout of a document).
- Audio technicians who work on audio bugs, telephone taps, and visual surveillance systems.
- Tech ops officers who work on tracking devices and sensors, weapons training and analysis, and special-use batteries. They also analyze foreign espionage equipment to figure out how it works (and use any good ideas they haven't developed already!).
- Tech ops officers who focus on creating disguises and counterfeit documents, such as travel documents and other official papers.

Since the days of World War II, these intelligence officers have been responsible for some cool gadgets, including:

- *The buttonhole camera*, which is concealed in an ordinary-looking coat. The lens, tucked behind a coat button, was perfectly positioned for photographing unsuspecting people. To take a picture, the person wearing the coat squeezed a shutter cable hidden in the coat pocket. Squeezing the cable caused the fake button to open and snap a picture.

- *The time-delay pencil*, a copper tube that contained a corrosive liquid, a copper wire, and a firing pin. It could be used to set off bombs.

- *The tear-gas pen*, which could be carried in a pocket or a purse. It looked just like a pen, but you wouldn't want to try to write with it by mistake. It shot out strong tear gas, which could be used to send your opponent into a coughing, eye-watering fit.

- *The jack-in-the-box,* or JIB, a flat, wooden figure that could be propped up in the passenger seat of a car. This would fool anyone who was following the car into thinking there was someone sitting next to the driver. The JIB was constructed to fit inside a briefcase. The driver could unlatch the briefcase with one hand, and the JIB would pop up into view.

- *The grit drill*, which solved a problem for spies who wanted to drill a hole in someone's plaster wall in order to place a bug. Ordinary drills always left a big clue: fine dust from the plaster. A tech ops officer created a drill that had a hose and vacuum-cleaner bag attached so the drill would, in a sense, clean up after itself.

- *The wristwatch camera*, which looked like an ordinary watch. However, it had a viewfinder, a shutter release, and a piece of film with six exposures. A spy could take a photo while pretending to check the time.

SPY SPEAK

Lemon squeezers:

Chemists who work on secret writing techniques. They adopted this name because lemon juice was one of the earliest forms of invisible ink. (If you hold a piece of paper over a heat source, such as a candle, the lemon juice will turn brown and you can read it.) During the Revolutionary War, George Washington was known to use, and to train his agents to use, invisible-writing techniques.

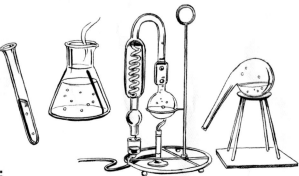

COVCOM:

An acronym for "covert communications," such as the group that develops methods—such as secret writing, short-range radio, subminiature cameras, special film, high-frequency broadcasts, satellite communications, and microdots—to talk or leave messages in secret.

Smile, You're on Candid Camera!

Over the years, spy cameras have become so small, they can be hidden in a number of unusual places, or in everyday devices such as your cell phone. So watch out—you never know who is taking your picture!

Here are a few places where cameras have been hidden to take secret snapshots:

- a cigarette pack
- a book
- a necktie
- a button
- a pair of sunglasses
- a glove
- a radio
- a handbag
- a wristwatch
- a matchbox
- a cigarette lighter
- a small statue
- a fountain pen

What kinds of people make good tech officers?

Obviously, people who love to tinker with electronic devices and enjoy figuring out how things work will do well in this area. Anyone who wants to use his or her tech skills for espionage also needs to be an extremely creative thinker. The problems you face as an intelligence officer are seldom covered in standard engineering textbooks.

For example, the spy who ends up using your gadget will probably be under some stress, so the directions can't be complicated. She may be trying to use it while under surveillance, so there can't be too many buttons to push. Not only should the gadget be small, but it would also be helpful if it could be operated while out of sight—say, in someone's coat pocket. And the gadget should need as little power as possible, since it's very inconvenient to run to the store for batteries in the middle of an operation!

You also have to be willing to try, try again—even when your new gizmo keeps failing. You never know when the break-through will come or what kind of vital intelligence might be uncovered through your work.

Do tech officers get stuck working in a lab all day?

Not at all! In fact, many tech officers travel around the world, working closely with case officers to develop the gadgets they need for particular missions. They are also often given the job of installing listening devices or secret cameras, which can involve missions as dramatic as anything you'd see in *Mission: Impossible.*

A story from the 1970s is a good example. One moonless night, two tech officers dressed in black had to crawl over slate roofs several stories above the ground to collect data. Using what looked like a small pistol that emitted radio waves, the officers measured the depths of several chimneys. With that information, they were able to make listening devices of precisely the right length to dangle inside the chimneys. A few weeks later, they had to repeat the mission, this time to install the microphones.

◉◉ Spy Story

In the early 1960s, CIA officers were trying to figure out how to eavesdrop on Soviet diplomats in a Central American country. The diplomats would hold their secret discussions in an outside courtyard under a tree, assuming that their offices were bugged.

Someone came up with the idea of putting a microphone and transmitter into a bullet, then firing the bullet into the tree! It wasn't hard to create a bugging device small enough to fit inside a bullet, but coming up with one that would withstand the impact was much harder.

The tech officers used a World War I rifle to test the bullet bug. They couldn't use a regular silencer on the vintage weapon, so they came up with the idea of having two motorcyclists start their engines as the gun was fired, to mask its sound. After doing many tests, they came up with a bullet bug that worked when fired into a block of plywood. Unfortunately, when they tried out the gadget with an actual tree, they discovered that the wood fibers interfered with the audio.

In the end, the bullet bug was a good idea that didn't work well enough to be used. However, the techies did create a rugged microphone that could stand up to very rough treatment—a useful innovation in itself!

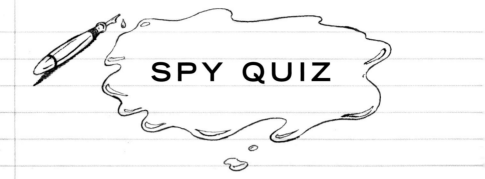

SPY QUIZ

What Kind of Spy Are You?

1) **Your friend, an avid soccer player, asks you to go to a party with a group of her teammates. You aren't athletic at all and have never watched a soccer game. You agree to go:**
   a) But spend the whole party sitting quietly by yourself as the other people chat about soccer.
   b) And spend the whole party talking to people, asking them questions about soccer and learning more about why they like the game so much.
   c) And then quiz the soccer players about how much force they use to kick the ball and how they calculate the trajectory of each shot.

2) **Your social studies teacher has given everyone an assignment to write about the history of your town. You:**
   a) Set up appointments to interview the mayor, the head of a local museum, and older people who have lived in the town for a long time.

b) Spend hours in the library, reading local history books and checking out census reports and blogs on the Internet.

c) Do a Google search to find someone who wrote an extensive history of your town. When you discover that the author has moved away, you talk to everyone to find someone who can help you get in touch with him.

3) You have a crush on a new kid at your school, but you don't know how to approach him or her. You:

a) Talk to people who have already made friends with your crush and find out what his or her interests are, then use that information to strike up a conversation.

b) Find out what your crush's interests are by observation, picking up on details such as what he or she talks about in class. You then go to the library and research those interests, and (this is the hard part) strike up a conversation.

c) Check your crush's Facebook page, then use what you've read to start talking.

4) It's the first week of a new school year, and all the students go to the gym to sign up for extracurricular activities. You:

a) Sign up for at least a dozen clubs and activities, including the tennis team, the drama club, the chess club, and the debate team—you love meeting new people and learning new things!

b) You don't sign up for any club but eventually decide you might be interested in the computer club. After all, you love doing research on the Internet, and your two best friends have already signed up.

c) Forget that this is the day to sign up for clubs, and go home early.

5) Your parents drag you to the wedding of some relative you don't know at all. You:

a) Make the best of the situation by making friends with all the cousins who are about your age and organizing a touch football game after the ceremony.

b) Sit in a corner at the reception with your nose buried in a book that you brought along—just in case you were bored.

c) Fall asleep during the wedding and start snoring, which embarrasses your parents and makes everyone laugh.

Answers

1) If you checked *a*, you might be a good analyst: You're not too comfortable talking to new people. But if you answered *b*, you might make a good case officer. You're outgoing and curious about other people; you like to hear about their interests and hobbies. If you answered *c*, you're definitely DS&T material.

2) If you checked *a*, you're outgoing and willing to talk to people, so you'd be a good case officer. If you checked *b*, you clearly like to find information in books and online; you'd be a great analyst. If you checked *c*, you could be good in either job—you have the analytical skills to track someone down and the people skills to figure out how to approach that person.

3) If you answered *a*, you have the people skills and the outgoing personality of a case officer. If you answered *b*, you're more of the analyst type. And if you answered *c*, you might have a career in the tech field ahead of you.

4) If you checked *a*, you're definitely the case officer type— you love being around people and making new friends. If you checked *b*, you're more of an analyst. You like research-oriented work and hanging with people you

already know well. If you checked *c* . . . well, you probably need to work on your organizational skills before you even think of becoming a spy!

5) If you checked *a*, you're a case officer, always ready to enjoy any new situation. If you checked *b*, you're an analyst, the kind of person who prefers reading a familiar book to meeting a room full of strangers. And if you checked *c*, you probably wouldn't be a good spy—after all, the first rule of spying is that you shouldn't attract attention to yourself!

HOW DO YOU BECOME A SPY?

I f you've read this far, you're probably pretty interested in becoming a spy. That leads to one big question: How, exactly, do you land this job? Surely it's not as easy as writing up a résumé and sending it to Washington, D.C.?

You're right, it's a little more complicated than that. But getting a job at an intelligence agency does start, like every other career, with a résumé and an interview. It's just that your interview with the CIA will be a little more detailed and challenging than your interview at the local burger joint!

Also, people with certain kinds of backgrounds will make better candidates. Read on to find out how you can prepare for the most top-secret job interview of your life!

Keep Quiet!

This warning is posted on the CIA Web site for anyone who wants to apply for a job.

Important Notice: Friends, family, individuals, or organizations may be interested to learn that you are an applicant for, or an employee of, the CIA. Their interest, however, may not be benign or in your best interest. You cannot control whom they would tell. We therefore ask you to exercise discretion and good judgment in disclosing your interest in a position with the Agency. You will receive further guidance on this topic as you proceed through your CIA employment processing.

WHO IS QUALIFIED TO BE A SPY?

First, anyone who works in intelligence should be, well, intelligent. If you're not a total brainiac, don't worry—you may be gifted with social intelligence (the ability to get along well with others). Still, you have to have a wide-ranging curiosity, a willingness to work hard, and a deep love of your country. If you like to be in the spotlight, you should probably look into another line of work—after all, a spy's biggest successes are often the terrible things that never happen, and you won't get much credit for those!

Second, you need to be an American citizen to work in the U.S. intelligence community (makes sense, right?).

Third, there are sometimes age limits for applicants that vary from one agency to another. (The best thing to do is check each agency's Web site for that information.) After all, the government is going to invest a lot of time and money training you, so they want you to be young enough to work for them for a while. Keep in mind, however, that if you have a specialty that's in demand, age and other requirements might well be waived in order to hire you.

Finally, you must have at least an undergraduate college degree with a grade point average of B or higher (so keep studying hard!). For many jobs in the intelligence community, a master's degree or PhD is required as well.

Does it matter what you study in school?

Yes and no. Intelligence agencies look for bright candidates; the field of study isn't as important as top grades. However, a person who has majored in one of the following areas will often have a leg up when it comes to getting hired:

- Biosciences
- Chemistry
- Computer science
- Economics
- Engineering
- Foreign languages
- Mathematics
- Military history
- Physics
- Political science
- World history

Do I have to speak a foreign language?

It definitely helps! Any kind of foreign language expertise is a big plus, whether you've studied the typical languages (French, Spanish, and German) or more exotic tongues. It's also true that if you know one foreign language, learning others is usually easier. But if you *really* want to improve your chances of working for an intelligence agency, start learning one of these languages—they're the most-needed languages today:

- Arabic
- Chinese
- Farsi
- Hindi
- Indic
- Japanese
- Korean
- Russian
- Turkish

HOW DO YOU APPLY FOR A JOB IN INTELLIGENCE?

Check out the Web site of each intelligence agency. They allow you to apply online!

I've heard you have to take a lie detector test as part of the job interview. Is that true?

Yes, it is, certainly at the CIA and FBI. If you've applied and been found to have the right stuff to be a spy, you'll have to go through an intensive background check. They'll do all the standard stuff, such as double-checking that you really did get that A+ in physics and that you actually did graduate, of course. But beyond that, any intelligence agency will want to check out how trustworthy, reliable, and honest you are—and how good you are at keeping secrets.

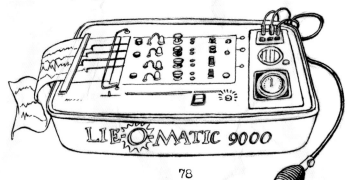

LIE-O-MATIC 9000

To do that, they may interview friends and neighbors. They could also ask you to take a lie detector test. They'll certainly ask you questions about your life, including any brushes with the law or drug use. And after all that, you'll have to take a physical to make sure that you're fit, both mentally and physically, for the job.

What are the different kinds of intelligence jobs available?

There are five areas of employment in most intelligence agencies:

Clandestine Service: The job titles may be rather boring—operations officer, staff operations officer, collection management officer—but don't be fooled! "Clandestine" means secret, and these people recruit spies.

Analysis: As discussed in the previous chapter, these employees take the raw information supplied by case officers and research and write reports for top-level officials, such as the president. People who work in this area often have studied economics, history, politics, or a specific world region, such as Europe or the Middle East.

Technology: If you love the idea of inventing spy gadgets, delving into computers, or working with spy satellites, this is the area for you! The engineers and scientists who work in technology are constantly researching and developing new ways of gathering and sorting information. (Plus, you may be assigned to create the next-generation wristwatch camera!)

Language: Intelligence agencies need people to translate documents, teach other employees a language, and keep on top of what's being reported around the world in foreign language newspapers and television shows.

Professional: Just like any huge company, an intelligence agency needs people who keep the organization running smoothly. This category includes everyone from secretaries to human resource officers, from day-care workers to janitors, and from paralegals to architects.

Can I get college assistance if I'm interested in a career in intelligence?

Some agencies offer internships and scholarships, which are listed on their Web sites.

⊙⊙ Spy Story

During the Cold War, anyone who visited the American ambassador's Moscow residence was handed a card to read, which said:

"Every room is monitored by the KGB and all of the staff are employees of the KGB. We believe the garden also may be monitored. Your luggage may be searched two or three times a day. Nothing is ever stolen and they hardly disturb things."

In other words, welcome . . . to the world of spies!

CHAPTER 5

SPY TRAINING

ongratulations! You got the job! If you've been hired as a case officer, you're probably raring to go . . . ready to steal secrets, recruit agents, and generally give James Bond a run for his money.

But hold on. There's a lot to learn about spying: how to follow somebody without getting caught, how to give the slip to people who are tailing you, how to pass secret messages to an agent, how to plant a bug . . . the list goes on and on.

That's where the Farm comes in. The Farm is the CIA's training ground in Virginia, where case officers go through about six months of training (the exact location and length of training are classified). The course is tough—among other things, you have to spend a few days in a swamp trying to escape from people who are hunting you down! There's also a jail sequence, where you're put in a jail, deprived of necessities, and interrogated.

Not all the classes are that strenuous, though. You also learn how to conduct and avoid surveillance, gather information at parties, recruit agents, write reports, set up secret meetings, use communications gadgets, secretly open and reseal letters, pick locks, take photos without being caught, create disguises, drive defensively, handle a weapon, and much more.

It may be a few years before you start to study at the Farm, so here's a sneak peek at what you'll learn if you become a spy someday!

 # SPY SPEAK

Tradecraft:
Espionage techniques and tricks—in other words, everything a spy needs to know to do his or her job!

How to keep someone under surveillance

Conducting surveillance is critical for a counterintelligence officer who is trying to catch people spying against our country. When you're secretly following (tailing) someone, in intelligence work you are surveilling them or conducting surveillance. As a new counterintelligence officer, you'll be told:

- Carry a few items with you—such as a hat, sunglasses, or an extra jacket—that you can use to change your appearance.

Even the most unobservant person might notice if you pop up nearby several times in one day. But they might not realize that the girl with brown hair at the deli counter is now the girl wearing a baseball cap on a street corner.

- If you're tailing someone day after day and your target follows a set routine, you're in luck! Rather than follow them step-by-step every day, you can pick them up at different points along their route so they're less likely to notice you.

- If your subject has a car or motorcycle, you'll learn how to attach a tracking device to the vehicle. It's a lot easier (and less noticeable) to track someone from a remote location than to jump in a cab and yell, "Follow that car!"

- Carry binoculars if you can. The reason? If you get too close to your subject, he or she is more likely to spot you. Binoculars allow you to hang back and still keep your target in sight.

- If you're spotted three times by your subject, give up. This is called being burned. Another way to say it? Game over.

HOW TO SPOT SURVEILLANCE

Although you may be asked to conduct surveillance as a counterintelligence officer (or "CI officer," or sometimes "counterspy"), you're more likely to be worried about other people following you. If someone is keeping you in his sights, you might not notice it, especially if several people are taking turns watching you. However, a good intelligence officer learns certain techniques for spotting the spies on his trail.

First, spies learn to look for patterns in their daily lives. When a pattern is disrupted, it means they need to pay attention— something may be wrong! When you go to spy school, you learn to notice the people around you. Usually, as you walk or drive through a city, people will come and go around you. If you notice someone who keeps popping up—sometimes behind you, sometimes in front of you—that's a good sign you're being followed.

For example, take a look at that blond woman wearing the beige raincoat—wasn't she behind you in line at the grocery store an hour ago? It seems unlikely that your paths would cross again.

The best way to learn how to spot such tails is to practice. Spies in training are sent out on practice runs to see if they can pick up on the person who's following them. Here are a few ways to figure out if you're really being followed and then shake the tail:

- As you're strolling along, casually make a right turn. If the person you suspect is still behind you, make another right turn. If she's still behind you, that's a good sign that she has you under surveillance.
- You can also make a U-turn. If your tail follows you, it's highly likely he's watching you.

- Drop a scrap of paper. If someone picks it up, that person probably has an unusually high interest in you, to say the least. (How many times do you collect other people's litter?)

Once you've figured out that you're being followed, what do you do? Many times, spies just keep going about their business. Now that they know they have a tail, they can keep the other guy in sight as long as he's still following. (You shouldn't assume, of course, that only one person is watching you!)

It's also important not to suspect everyone around you of being a spy. This is what's known as "seeing ghosts." You're already a little jumpy because of your job, and you know there's a good chance someone's following you, so you start to see surveillance everywhere.

After all, if you look at anyone with suspicion, they start to seem, well . . . suspicious! That old man with a cane? How do you know he's not a young man wearing a gray wig? That woman carrying three shopping bags? How do you know she doesn't have a camera hidden in one of the bags to secretly film you? That college student riding a skateboard and listening to an MP3 player? How do you know the MP3 player isn't a secret transmission device?

Experience and good training can help a spy learn to overcome this reaction. After a while, many spies develop a gut instinct for whether someone is real or a plant. Still, it's good to remember—just because you haven't spotted someone watching you doesn't mean no one's there!

How to work while under surveillance

What if you know you're under surveillance, but you have an important document that you're supposed to give to someone? You don't want your tail to see you handing off the papers, obviously. In this kind of situation, spies learn how to pass near one another and covertly hand off a small package or packet of material, this is also known as doing a "brush pass": As you walk past the person who's supposed to get the papers, you manage to hand them over without your tail seeing you do so. Then you keep walking. If you did it right, your tail will still be following you because he didn't notice a thing! You may also try to do the brush pass in a passageway or just as you turn a corner, so the person following you is even less likely to see it.

SPY SPEAK

Surveillance:

All forms of observation or monitoring, from a person on the street tailing someone to a satellite in the sky taking photos from space.

Surveillant:

A person who watches or observes someone else.

SPY SPEAK

Brush pass:

A method of handing a document or object to another person without being seen; it involves passing near the other person, making an unobtrusive handoff, and then walking or driving on.

Car toss:

Another method of passing material. The case officer or agent leaves her car window down slightly so that someone walking by can inconspicuously toss material into the otherwise locked car. The car can be parked in a certain spot or in a certain position to indicate that the driver is ready to receive the material.

How to evade surveillance

Spies usually don't try to get away from their surveillants or surveillance teams immediately, since that's a dead giveaway that the tail has been spotted. Still, you may have to lose your follower at some point. How do you do that? Try these tricks:

- Go into an office building, walk through the lobby, and exit through another door.
- If you're driving, pretend to miss a turnoff, then circle around to get back on the right road.
- Stop and pretend to look at a map. Your followers will not be able to stop without alerting you to their presence.
- Duck into an alley or bathroom to execute a quick-change disguise by putting on (or taking off) accessories or items of clothing, such as eyeglasses, a raincoat, hat, or scarf, or by changing shoes.

HOW TO RECRUIT AGENTS

A case officer's job is to recruit agents—that is, persuade people to become spies. A case officer has to be patient, since it takes a long time to figure out if someone would make a good spy and then to win his or her trust. Here's one example of how to do that:

First, you have to figure out what secrets you want to get. Let's say you want to find out whether a foreign official—let's call him Mr. X—is knowledgeable about his country's preparations for war. You would make a list of people who are close to Mr. X. Your list might include people on his staff, his family and friends, and maybe even the night janitor who is allowed to come and go as he pleases (and who overhears conversations on a daily basis).

Second, you try to find out if any of these people seem like promising agents. Perhaps one of Mr. X's assistants feels he has been unfairly passed over for promotion. Let's call him Mr. Y. Maybe Mr. Y also owes a lot of money and needs to make some extra cash, fast.

Now that you've targeted a potential source, you find out everything you can about him or her. Perhaps you follow him for a few days. Maybe you chat with the doorman at his apartment building after asking for directions. You've learned enough to know that Mr. Y goes to his favorite restaurant several times a month, takes a weekly karate class at his gym, and spends occasional Saturdays in the park with his bird-watching club.

Then you arrange a meeting. If you know one of Mr. Y's friends or colleagues, you may be able to get them to introduce you. But perhaps you don't want to be so obvious—sometimes spies have to be subtle after all!

This is where your research comes in handy, because it will help you set up a seemingly chance meeting. For example, you could book a table at that restaurant and start a conversation by asking Mr. Y what dish he recommends. You could sign up for the karate class. Or you could join the bird-watching club.

Once you've met Mr. Y, you need to develop the relationship, just as you would anytime you meet a new person and want to become friends. Perhaps you suggest grabbing a bite to eat after karate. Then you follow up later with an invitation to the movies. Your conversations with Mr. Y are friendly, but you are always probing and trying to figure out if Mr. Y would make a good agent.

As people become friends, they naturally start to reveal more personal information. When Mr. Y tells you he's frustrated with his job, you draw him out. You ask him questions about that promotion he wanted. You're sympathetic and say you understand his disappointment.

Eventually, if you've decided Mr. Y could be a good agent, you need to feel him out about spying for you. This has to be done very carefully, of course—you don't want him to run back to Mr. X and tell him what you're doing!

But by now, you and Mr. Y are friends. He likes you. Plus, you offer to help him with his debt. If you've done a good job so far, you have a good chance of recruiting Mr. Y—and finally finding out what Mr. X has planned.

How to avoid being a recruitment target

There are many different ways to recruit agents, of course. This is something to keep in mind in case you're ever the object of a recruitment approach. For example, let's say a terrorist comes to the United States determined to place a bomb in a train station. He needs to know everything about security, train timetables, and traffic patterns. Perhaps you work at that station and he targets you as a potential source.

Do you think he'll tell you he's a terrorist and is planning to plant a bomb? Not likely! And do you think he'll look like everyone's idea of a wild-eyed terrorist? No way.

Instead, he may be dressed in a suit and tie. He may tell you he works for a government agency . . . say, the CIA. He may even flash a badge. (This is an old spy trick. If you know someone won't work for your country, you pretend to be on the side of a country that he *does* want to help. This is called a "false-flag recruitment.")

You're impressed, especially when he gives you some insider information. The CIA has heard rumors, he says, that this train station may be a terrorist target. He could use your help to stop any possible attacks. All you need to do is tell him if you notice a security officer who may have money problems, because those people could be recruited by the terrorists. Oh, and let him know if more people travel at certain times of day, since that might be when terrorists would want to detonate their bomb.

It's no trouble for you to find out this kind of information and pass it on. Plus, the idea of helping the CIA is kind of cool. You've always liked James Bond movies! And you're a patriotic person. You'd be proud to help keep your country safe.

You've taken the bait! But then this recruiter casually adds another incentive. He doesn't have a huge budget, he says, but he can offer a small amount of money for your help. How does five hundred dollars a month sound?

You can hardly believe it! That money will make a big difference in your life—and you hardly even have to work for it!

Later, when you discover the awful truth of who you're working for, you try to quit, but the recruiter points out that you've been paid to spy against your country and you're in too deep to get out now.

Of course, this doesn't mean you shouldn't help an intelligence officer if she asks for it! But you want to take a close look at that badge. And call her office to make sure she really works there!

 SPY SPEAK

False-flag recruitment:

When a spy recruits someone by pretending to be working for another group or agency (for example, if a CIA officer recruited an agent by pretending to be a KGB agent, he or she would be working under a false flag).

Witting:

A spy term meaning "in the know." For example, if the CIA is running an operation, one case officer might ask if another officer is witting, meaning, "Does he know about the operation?"

HOW TO TELL IF SOMEONE IS LYING

Let's say you're talking to someone who claims to have the inside scoop on a military coup that's about to take place in a foreign country. Do you believe him or not? A big part of a spy's job is learning how to assess other people. And the most basic assessment is this: Are you telling me the truth?

According to communications experts, there are a few things to look for to see whether someone is telling the truth. Most of the time, these telltale signs would appear during an official interrogation, which means that an average case officer wouldn't focus too intently on them. However, even a casual interview is a low-level interrogation of sorts, so it's good to have some working knowledge of these signs.

Common signs that someone is lying include:

- A change in the voice's pitch (it suddenly gets higher or lower than normal)
- A change in how fast or slow the person is talking or breathing
- A sudden increase in "ums" and "ers"
- A change in eye contact. (It's a common belief that people who won't look you in the eye are lying. In fact, some people don't gaze directly into their listeners' eyes because they're shy or because it's considered rude in their culture. However, most people make eye contact around half the time. If there's a sudden difference in how often someone is looking at you, it may be a sign that that person is fudging a bit.)

- Turning away from you, even if it's only a slight change of body position
- A widening of the eyes, so that you can see the white at the top and bottom
- Covering the mouth with a hand, even briefly
- Nervously moving feet or legs
- A mismatch between body language and what is being said. For example, if someone says he likes you, but his fist is clenched—watch out! Or if someone is smiling with her mouth but not her eyes, that may be a sign that she's forcing the smile for a reason.

- An overuse of phrases like "to tell you the truth" and "to be perfectly honest." People who are telling the truth don't keep insisting that they're, well, telling the truth!
- Keeping hands unnaturally still. People normally use hand gestures when they're talking in order to make a point. When they start to lie, however, they stop moving their hands.
- Constantly asking you to repeat your questions, which may be a way of stalling while figuring out how to come up with a convincing lie.
- Using the words of your question to form his answer. For example, if you ask, "Did you steal the top secret document from the senator's office?" his answer might be, "No, I did not steal the top secret document from the senator's office."

HOW TO CREATE A COVER

As a spy, you're constantly pretending to be someone else— it's just part of the job description. The part you play is called your cover identity. In order to create your identity, you have to develop a detailed biography of the person you're supposed to be. This background story is called your legend.

You also have to do research so that you know your part perfectly. Otherwise, you might get tripped up by something simple, like forgetting the name of a large department store in your hometown, and blow your cover.

The research that goes into creating a legend can be quite detailed. For example, here are some of the questions you'll need to have answers to:

- **Where did you grow up?** No matter what town you pick, you'd better know all about it—after all, what if you happen to meet someone from that town who wants to talk about the great candy store on Main Street, or the championship high school football team? Fortunately, you can learn a lot about a place on the Internet. Even small newspapers often have a Web site where you can read through hundreds of articles, going back to the years when you supposedly lived there. (Tip: If you do get caught in a conversation about your hometown, change the subject as quickly as possible or say that you moved away when you were young.)
- **Where did you go to school and what did you study?** Again, if you claim to have gone to a certain college, you'd better know all about its campus. If you say you majored in geology, you'd better know the difference between sandstone and granite.
- **What do you do now?** This is where you really must know your stuff. You need to be able to use the right kind of jargon for your job—a taxi driver may use different words than a professor for the same things.
- **Why are you here?** There needs to be a believable reason for your presence, whether in a foreign country or at an embassy party.

Once you've created your new identity, you're ready to take it on the road. Here are little touches that will make your disguise more believable:

- **Pocket litter:** This is the term for the identification cards, credit cards, photographs, and other scraps of paper and small objects that we all keep in our wallets, purses, briefcases, pockets, and luggage.

  Just a small example: If your cover is that you're an opera buff, you might have the stub of a ticket to *Carmen* in your pocket (and the ticket better match where you claim to have been on that date!). If you said that you recently traveled from another country, you might still have a few coins from that country. If you claim that you've been living in a particular neighborhood for the last month, you probably will have a few receipts from a local dry cleaner or bookstore.

- **Props:** Think about the character you've created. What kind of clothes would he wear? Probably a tailored suit if he's a business executive, or jeans and a T-shirt if he's a student. What kind of props would he carry? A platinum credit card for the executive, or a worn backpack for the student. If your character is an internationally known scientist, should she carry the latest scientific journal in her briefcase? If he's a famous fashion designer, what kind of trendy cell phone should he carry—and whose names and numbers should be on speed dial? You can add more and more details, from how expensive your haircut should be to whether your shoes should be shined or scuffed. The more carefully you plan your look, the more likely people will be to believe your story.

Cover identity:

The fake identity you take on as a spy. This may be your official or nonofficial cover job in your city of assignment. It could also be an identity with a cover that you take on for a special operation in another city or country.

Legend:

The detailed background you create to support your cover story.

Pocket litter:

What you carry in your pockets—such as receipts, notes, and coins—that makes your cover more believable.

HOW TO WORK UNDERCOVER

When you're working undercover, you need to become the other person. That doesn't mean you have to change your voice or your personality. But you do have to think about what you would wear, where you would go, and what you would be interested in if you really were the person you're pretending to be.

For example, perhaps you're posing as a writer. This is actually a great cover for a spy, since writers often travel around the world to do research and usually have to ask a lot of questions. It's difficult, on the other hand, to take on the cover of an engineer if you don't have a technical background. If you strike up a conversation with someone and they start asking questions about your job, they'll probably know you're lying very quickly.

So, let's say your cover is being a writer. You're probably going to be casually dressed. You wouldn't wear a tie, for example. If you're a man, you might let your hair grow a little longer. You need to act like a writer and do what a writer might do. You would probably hang out at bookstores. If you're supposed to be someone who writes about culture, you might visit museums. Writers often don't make a lot of money, so you would probably meet people at a local coffee shop instead of the hottest new restaurant.

All those places that it would be natural for you to visit would also be good places to meet contacts or set up a dead drop. On the other hand, it would be unnatural for you to visit the local ammunitions plant or military base (unless you write about military affairs). However, you could go into the American embassy to supposedly renew your passport, and use that visit to pass on information. Even when you're inside the embassy, though, you need to remember that some of the staff might actually be locals who are paid to watch what goes on and report to your opposition. So your role always has to be consistent when you're working undercover. There could be many eyes watching you, so you always have to act as if you're onstage.

How to spot bugs and hidden cameras

When you're a spy, you've got to assume: Someone is always watching. Or listening. Or both.

As a spy, you plant your fair share of bugs and set up a number of hidden cameras. You know your competition is doing the same thing to you.

So here are some tips for spotting those little cameras and microphones before they spot you:

- Check out anything that doesn't work. Is the fan in your room broken? Is the light in the hotel hallway never turned on? Those may be fake fixtures that are used for bugs and cameras.
- Examine the mirror in your hotel bathroom. Put your face up close, hold your hands to shield your eyes from the light, and try to look through it. If it's a two-way mirror with a camera behind it, you should be able to see it.
- Look for little holes drilled into the wall or ceiling that could be a sign of electronic surveillance—or a bad handyman. (Tip: If someone has drilled holes in your wall, they may have left some telltale sawdust behind.)
- Check behind the ventilation or air-conditioning grill.

How to plant a bug

Thanks to technological advances, bugs are tinier than ever. Just think: In 1946, a bug was the size of a balled-up fist. But by the 1990s, a bug was slightly smaller than an olive! They can be placed in almost any object, including clocks, calculators, radios, watches, cigarette lighters, furniture, books, cans of shaving cream, and desk lamps.

However, sneaking into a room to plant a bug can still pose real risk. Tech officers are often given this job, so they have to be ready with a cover story to explain why they're in the office or room where they're planting the bug.

Fortunately, it's not always necessary to get inside the room you're bugging. Sometimes the only access you need is a pinhole for a wire that is connected to the bug. For example, you could get into the room next door to the one you actually want to bug, and then drill a tiny hole into the baseboard or even through the wall. Once you put the wire into that hole, the transmitter will pick up the sound waves created when people talk.

How to counter a bug

If you think your room is bugged but you still need to talk to someone, the easiest way to foil your enemies is to turn on a radio or TV. The noise will mask your conversation. But even this isn't foolproof—tech officers can often figure out ways to filter out the radio or TV noise in order to hear what's being said.

Another way to avoid electronic eavesdropping is to go outside. But even then, telescope microphones have been developed that can be aimed at people from some distance away in order to pick up their conversations.

Even if you think you've found every bug and have turned up the radio or strolled out into the backyard, be careful what you say—every intelligence organization has a team of clever tech officers who are trying to figure out how to counter your tricks. And if you think you're safe, that's even better for them, since you'll be less likely to guard your tongue!

👓 Spy Story

In 1946, the Russians wanted to bug the American embassy in Moscow. Great idea—but how could they get into the embassy to plant a listening device?

The answer: They created a carved wooden replica of the Great Seal of the United States and placed the bug inside it. Then they had a group of Russian schoolchildren present the seal to the American ambassador. He accepted it graciously and hung it on a wall in his office. Since the device did not require any external power source to function (it was a so-called passive cavity resonator that had no wires), it could run indefinitely. The Americans discovered it six years later during a routine security check.

👓 Spy Story

Spies must be able to think of clever solutions to unusual problems. For example, a team of tech officers was given the assignment of bugging a building in an African country. They knew that they had to slip into the building at night, while it was empty, and that they would have to do extensive drilling before installing the wires and microphones.

The problem: What would the neighbors think? After all, the building was supposed to be empty at night. People were sure to start asking questions if they heard the drills.

After tossing around a few ideas for covering up the sound, the chief offered a strange solution: bullfrogs.

The other officers were confused until he explained. There were lots of bullfrogs in the area, and they made a lot of noise at night. The station chief asked his staff to collect several sacks of bullfrogs and let them loose around the building before the operation was scheduled to take place. Sure enough, the bullfrogs croaked away—and none of the neighbors noticed a thing!

👓 Spy Story

One legendary CIA story tells of a South American dictator who discovered a transmitter hidden in a piece of wood on his desk. Enraged, he pulled out a pistol and shot the piece of wood several times, while yelling to his staff about the CIA and the United States. Then he dramatically tossed the bullet-ridden piece of wood to the top of his filing cabinet and forgot about it, his point made.

However, none of the bullets had actually destroyed the transmitter! For the next several weeks, the bug continued to record every word said in the dictator's office, until the batteries finally died.

How to make and use a dead drop

Many times, case officers would rather not be seen meeting face-to-face with their agents. But what if they have to hand over secret documents or get a necessary gadget, such as a minicamera, or pass on some money?

In those instances, the case officer sets up a signal site to let her fellow agent know she has something to deliver. The signal could be a chalk mark on a certain bench, a crumpled soda can left at a predetermined spot, or a string tied around a certain lamppost. She could also signal from her apartment by hanging a colored towel over a railing or moving a potted plant from one window to another.

Next, the case officer sets up a dead drop. This is a predetermined location where something can safely be concealed for a later pickup.

When something is put in the dead drop, it's called loading the drop. When something is picked up, it's called unloading the drop.

As you might imagine, finding the perfect spot for a dead drop is harder than it seems. Here are some things you need to keep in mind. The dead drop location should:

- Be hidden from casual onlookers. That means you shouldn't pick a spot next to an apartment building, where lots of people could look out the window or see what you're doing. It's also best to avoid places that attract a lot of people, such as dog walkers, parents with strollers, kids at play, and so on.

- Be accessible regardless of the weather. You really don't want to have to dig through three feet of snow to pick up that dandy new eavesdropping device, do you? We didn't think so.

- Be accessible at any time. What if you can't get to the dead drop until midnight? You can't use an office building, since it's locked up for the night. And if you need to make pickups during the day, you might also want to avoid using a nightclub, which doesn't open until the evening.

- Allow you to check for surveillance. If there are a lot of hiding spots around the dead drop, you'll have no way of knowing whether you're being watched.

- Fit in with your cover. For example, if you're posing as a chef, then the dead drop could be outside a grocery store.

Once you've found the perfect location, you need to:

- Figure out a safe way to get there without attracting attention.

- Make up a cover story for why you're there, just in case the worst happens and someone does ask.

- Put the item you're handing off in a waterproof container or wrap it in plastic. In some cases, spies put their messages inside concealment devices, such as a fake rock. The concealment device should be something that no one would want to pick up, such as a crumpled soda can or a dirty garbage bag. (All used food containers, such as soda cans, should be washed thoroughly before being used, to keep wild animals from carrying them off—another spy trick!)

- Leave your signal that you've made the dead drop and hope that everything works as planned.

◎◎ Spy Story

Perhaps the most original (and grossest) concealment device was a fake pile of dog poop containing a hollow space. No one was likely to pick that up!

Other seemingly ordinary objects—such as a pipe, dirty mitten, dead rat, discarded milk carton, or plastic tube— have also been used as hiding spots.

SPY SPEAK

Dead drop:

A predetermined location where something can safely be concealed for later pickup by a contact. The CIA uses the term "dead drop." The Russians call this method of handing off information *taynik*. The British refer to a dead drop as a "dead letter box."

◉◉ Spy Story

During the Cold War, a case officer needed a fake brick to use as a dead drop. He planned to put money inside the brick and leave it near a transmission tower outside of Moscow for an agent to pick up. Intelligence officers working in Moscow collected pieces of brick from the area so the tech officer could match the color and texture. After working long hours in his lab, the tech officer presented his fake brick.

It looked perfect—until another officer picked it up.

It felt as light as a Styrofoam brick!

The techie had to go back to the lab and try again.

A few months later, the Soviet agent was told to go to the dead drop site and pick up the brick with his money. He followed his instructions to the letter—but when he picked up the brick, he thought he must have gotten them wrong. After all, this brick looked and felt exactly like a real brick. It couldn't be a fake!

He tossed it to the ground and went home, only to be told several days later to go back to the site. That brick, which had looked and felt so real, was the fake.

Fortunately, it was still there, and he was able to get his money—and the tech officer knew his work was so good that it even fooled someone who knew what he was looking for!

How to deal with codes and ciphers

First, you have to learn the difference between a code and a cipher. A code is a word or phrase that you use when you mean something else. For example, maybe you're sitting at a cafeteria table and someone is talking on and on about the auditions for the school play. The only problem is that you have zero interest in drama. You say to your friend, "I really wish I had a bologna sandwich." He knows that what you really mean is, "Let's get out of here and do something fun before lunch period is over." That's because you and your best friend had agreed that your code word for "I'm bored" was—you guessed it!—"bologna."

A cipher, on the other hand, is a way to send secret messages by replacing one letter with another. For example, you and your friend might agree that you will write messages by transposing every letter three spaces to the left. So, in this case:

A = D	N = Q
B = E	O = R
C = F	P = S
D = G	Q = T
E = H	R = U
F = I	S = V
G = J	T = W
H = K	U = X
I = L	V = Y
J = M	W = Z
K = N	X = A
L = O	Y = B
M = P	Z = C

If this is the cipher you and your friend agree upon, he might pass you a message that reads: LP VR ERUHG!

How to brief your bosses, all the way up to the president of the United States

When you're conducting a briefing, remember to be clear and accurate and get to the point. Sometimes analysts know so much about their subject that they want to present too much information. It's important to have your thoughts in order and present only the information that is absolutely necessary.

When a new president is sworn into office, the intelligence agencies try to get a sense of how the new president wants to get information. For example, President Jimmy Carter was formerly a naval submarine commander. Anyone in that position has to know what every nut and bolt on the submarine is meant to do; as a result, President Carter wanted lots of details.

When President Ronald Reagan was in office, the CIA would sometimes make videos to brief him. When he was going to meet with Palestinian leader Yasser Arafat, for example, the CIA created a minidocumentary about who Arafat was, where he came from, and what he believed.

The first rule of presentation is, "Understand your audience." When your audience is the president of the United States, you have to spend time figuring out the best way to present to him or her.

How to assess a walk-in

Sometimes a person will walk into an American embassy, phone someone, or walk up to an American official and—completely out of the blue—volunteer to pass on secret information. These people are called walk-ins.

When this happens, you need to figure out, as quickly as possible, how genuine you think the individual is. After all, he could be a "dangle" (or even a possible double agent).

SPY SPEAK

Dangle:

A person is "dangled" in front of an intelligence service by a rival intelligence service in hopes he may learn about the service, how it works, its requirements, its officers, and other information. The dangle may even pretend to be recruited while remaining loyal to those who dangled him. In this case he would be a double agent, namely, someone pretending to work for one intelligence service but really working for the service that dangled him.

There are three things you need to figure out:

- Why is the person offering his help? The simplest motive is greed; he wants to be paid for his information. However, the walk-in might be a patriot who is dismayed by what is happening in her country. A less noble motive might be revenge; sometimes military or intelligence officers who work for other countries are passed over for promotion and decide to betray their country because they feel disgruntled. And sometimes the walk-in just has a big ego and feels a sense of arrogance and satisfaction in secretly fooling all of her colleagues.

- How much access does the walk-in have? You have to figure out if she actually can get you the information she says she wants to pass on. Someone may say she has all kinds of insider knowledge about a foreign country's king or cabinet, but then you discover that everything she knows she read in the newspaper—just like everybody else!

- Finally, you need to determine if the walk-in has burned his bridges, or if he can keep working at his regular job. He might be a military officer who's privy to classified information about troop movements. If this is the case, and he is still working, you will try to persuade the walk-in to become a "defector in place." Rather than the usual defector, who flees his country and hands off any information he has, this person can continue living his normal life. The only difference is that now he can keep reporting to you, in real time, about everything that he sees and hears.

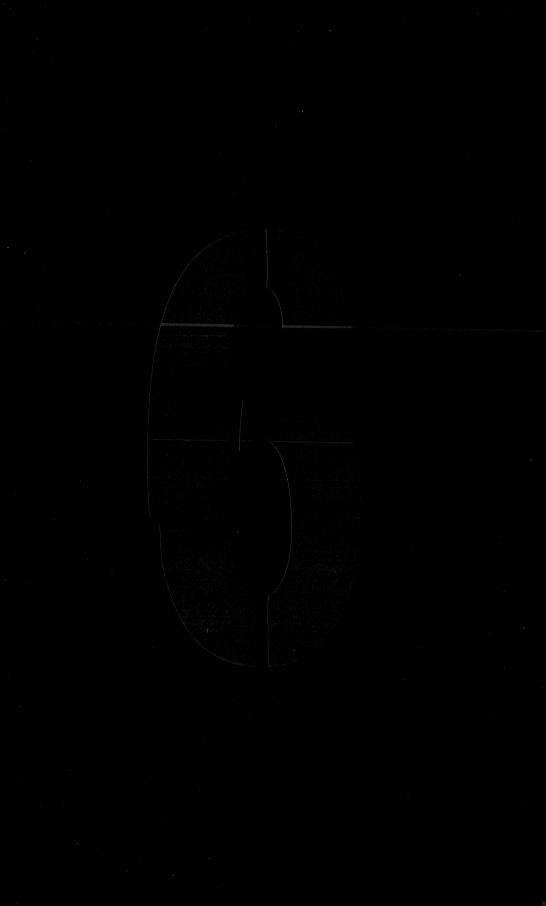

PRACTICE YOUR SPY SKILLS

Y ou don't have to wait until you're out of school to start to learn and practice many basic skills that would serve you well as a spy. Here are a few exercises to try—and remember, even if you don't end up working as an intelligence officer, many of these skills will help you in other exciting careers as well.

BE CURIOUS ABOUT THE WORLD

Let's say you are an intelligence analyst and you are assigned to France. The first thing you would do is study the major French media sources. That's because intelligence officers don't recruit (and pay) people to give them information if they can get it from open sources.

A good first step would be to read the newspaper every day. If you read it online, you'll also be able, in many cases, to take advantage of links to other sources of information and read newspapers from around the world. Many major news sites offer translations, so you're not limited to publications in English.

Be adventurous—try to read as many different points of view as possible. (Remember, the idea is to find out what is actually happening in the world, not what we wish was happening or what we think is happening from our Western perspective.)

At first, you might be a little overwhelmed by the amount of information. To make this exercise a little easier, pick one topic on which you'd like to become an expert. For example, you may want to know as much as possible about a conflict between two countries, the very latest computer technologies being developed, or a new political movement. Try to find out something new about your topic every day. To do this, you could:

- Read the newspaper every day, paying special attention to any new stories on your topic.

- Set up an automated alert to let you know when a new story is posted.
- Follow links in the news stories to get more information.

- Find magazine articles online that offer useful background information.
- Set up RSS feeds to blogs written by experts on your topic and have the news delivered to your e-mail inbox.
- Check out library books that cover your topic.
- Pretend you're an analyst who's been asked to write a report on your topic. How would you organize the information? Do you see any trends that you should point out? Write the report! (You might even get extra credit in one of your classes.) This will give you a taste of what it's like to sift through information and present it to someone else—such as the head of the CIA or the president of the United States!
- Find someone, perhaps an adult, who is also interested in a foreign country or a topic, like terrorism. Start exchanging ideas and even arguing about your mutual interest. If this seems a little odd, just think of how you debate with your friends about your favorite sports teams or movies, and bring that same passion to foreign policy issues!

Follow the Story

Here are a few news Web sites you can visit to learn more about what's going on in the world—a necessity for any good spy! But these sites should just be a starting point. Seek out your own sources, especially if you're interested in a particular part of the world. Many foreign language newspapers have English translations (or, if you're learning another language, you can practice by reading their regular pages).

AFP: www.afp.com/afpcom/en

Al Jazeera: english.aljazeera.net

Associated Press: www.ap.org

BBC: www.bbc.co.uk

CNN: www.cnn.com

C-SPAN: www.cspan.org

Foreign Policy: www.foreignpolicy.com

Los Angeles Times: www.latimes.com

Newsweek: www.newsweek.com

New York Times: www.nytimes.com

Reuters: www.reuters.com

Time: www.time.com/time

Washington Post: www.washingtonpost.com

Sites with links to newspapers and news shows around the world

ABYZ News Links: www.abyznewslinks.com

BeelineTV.com: beelinetv.com

The Internet Public Library: www.ipl.org/div/news

News and Newspapers Online: library.uncg.edu/news

Onlinenewspapers.com: www.onlinenewspapers.com

Refdesk.com: www.refdesk.com/paper.html

Voice of America: www.voanews.com/english/portal.cfm

Worldpress.org: www.worldpress.org

Work on your note-taking skills

You already have to take notes in class, right? It's a tricky skill to learn. How much of what your teacher says is important enough to write down? When should you stop writing and just listen? How can you organize your notes so they make sense?

And can you read your own handwriting a few days later when you're studying for a test? Have you gotten in the practice of typing up your notes so they are easier to review weeks or months later?

As a spy, you may have to take notes, too—sometimes late at night in a dark car parked in a remote area. Later, you may have to quickly organize those notes into a report. When you take notes in history class, imagine your teacher's lecture is actually intelligence that an asset is passing on to you. Listen carefully so you can write down the most important points. (Remember that spies, unlike students, can't always be seen taking notes, but they want to recall the main points about what they've heard. It's not unusual for a spy to pick up good information in a social setting and then go someplace private, often a bathroom, to quickly record the highlights of the information. This isn't an ideal situation, but it's often necessary.)

Then do what real spies do and write your report as soon as possible—that day, if you can. You may want to try retyping your notes on your computer so they'll be easier to read when you're studying. And organizing the notes will also help you remember what you learned—which will come in very handy when your teacher (or the president) announces a pop quiz!

Improve your writing

Once you've gathered intelligence, either from your asset or from open-source information, you have to write a report for your boss that tells him or her what you've found out. In fact, as a case officer, you might have to write a number of reports a week depending on how many agents have given you information. You'll also have to write under tight deadlines and the pressure of other work.

So don't groan when your history teacher gives your class the assignment of writing an essay. Think of it as useful practice for the day when you have to dash off five pages about the intelligence you've gathered that indicates that country A is about to invade country B.

Learn to make quick sketches

Words aren't always the best way to communicate what you've learned. What if you need to describe the layout of an army base or indicate where a secret pile of weapons is stashed? You might be in a situation where using a camera would jeopardize yourself and your mission. Case officers often use sketches and diagrams to brief colleagues and to tell agents where to leave secret information.

Work on your presentation skills

Actually, if you've just found out something really urgent—such as the news that one country is about to attack another—you might have to present your information in person. You might even be called into the Oval Office to tell the president what you know. In fact, junior analysts have often found themselves briefing senior policy makers and high-ranking foreign leaders because they were experts on a particular topic.

In that situation, you're going to want to be able to speak clearly (definitely avoid saying "um" or "you know"), be organized, and be prepared to answer tough, pointed questions about your topic and your analysis. You're also going to be a lot more nervous than when you have to give a book report or oral presentation in school.

Learn how to use maps, props, and presentation software to give presentations. The trick is to avoid giving a "data dump" to an audience. Remember, you know your subject inside and out. Sometimes analysts try to speak too fast and cram everything they know into a briefing or presentation, leaving their audience overwhelmed with information. A briefing is not about showing how much you know; it's about delivering a concise, clear presentation so that the audience grasps the essential points you wish to convey.

So use those horrible moments when you have to get up in front of your class to prepare for someday briefing your agency's director or even the president. Every little bit of practice helps!

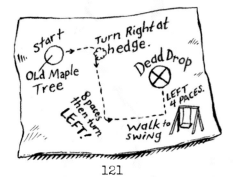

Learn a foreign language

If your school offers foreign language classes, take one! Knowing another language is one of the best ways to prepare for a life as a spy. Obviously, it's much easier to get information in another country if you speak the language (and it's much more fun to eavesdrop!). What's more, once you've learned one language, it's easier to learn others.

You can also research the different customs and practices in other countries. Pretend that you might be sent to that country and would need to operate undercover. How would you dress to fit in? What kinds of typical American behavior would you have to avoid so that you wouldn't blow your cover?

Improve your memory

You might complain about studying for tests at school. After all, memorizing dates for history class or the names of the planets can be kind of boring. But you might find your homework a little more fun if you treated each study session as a chance to practice being a spy.

Spies need to have excellent memories. They may meet with someone who is going to pass on vital information, but find that they can't take notes because it would attract attention and, if they were captured, would be evidence of spying.

What can they do? Listen as closely as possible, committing every detail to memory, then write notes on the conversation as soon as possible. Or a spy may be assigned to report back on what he sees at a naval shipyard or construction site in a foreign country. He obviously can't hang out in a secured area, taking photos and jotting down everything he sees! The only thing he can do is observe and memorize any activity that looks important.

One way to build your memory muscles is by creating a mnemonic (pronounced "ni-*mah*-nick"—the first *m* is not sounded out). That's a phrase, word, or mental image that helps you remember a key piece of information.

For example, let's say you're studying for a geography quiz and you can't remember how many lakes make up the Great Lakes. You might imagine a giant number five in bright red at the top of the map of the United States. And if you can't remember the names of the Great Lakes, you might use the word HOMES as a reminder. HOMES includes the first letter of the name of each lake: Huron, Ontario, Michigan, Erie, and Superior.

If you want to test yourself outside of school, try playing this game with a friend: collect a number of small objects, the more varied the better. For example, you might grab several coins, a piece of costume jewelry, a pencil, a paper clip, an eraser, several dominoes, a chess piece, a take-out menu, a flash drive, a magnet, a box of matches, a pebble, a business card, a buckle, and so on.

When your friend is out of the room, place five items on a table and cover them with a cloth. When he comes back in, take the cloth off the objects and let him study them for several minutes. Then cover the objects again and tell him to write a list of everything he saw. If you find that five objects is too easy, then add more each time you play. You can also give the player less time to memorize the objects, making the game even harder! This was a test that the author Rudyard Kipling described in his book *Kim*, about a young boy training to become a spy.

These exercises can develop your memory, but it's a little trickier to use mnemonics in real life since you have to make them up on the fly. However, it can be done, especially with some practice.

Take a common situation: You're chatting with someone at a party and she drops several interesting pieces of information in the course of the conversation. You can't whip out a notebook and jot down what she said! Instead, you might assign those pieces of information to the letters A, B, and C.

Perhaps the person you're talking to says that a certain country is sending weapons and tanks to another country, and that the man in charge of this operation is a certain general.

You might decide that A stands for "arms" (which helps you remember weapons).

B stands for "big cars" (which helps you remember tanks).

C stands for "colonel" (and, yes, the person in charge is a

general—but C makes you think of "colonel" and that reminds you of military officers and that takes you to the general you need to make note of).

Another classic memory aid is to imagine yourself walking through your house and to visualize an object in each room that stands for what you want to remember. For example, you might picture yourself opening the front door and stepping into the front hall, where you see a gun rack. That stands for "arms." As you turn right into the living room, you "see" a tank in front of the fireplace. And as you continue on to the kitchen, you visualize a man wearing a general's uniform sitting at the table.

Of course, as soon as you can, you would excuse yourself, hurry to the bathroom, and jot down these notes—using your memory aids—so you can make sure you don't forget all the important information you've so carefully visualized.

Practice your social skills

A good case officer recruits assets by being friendly, since it's hard to convince someone to give secrets to another country if that person doesn't like you. You may think you're already a pretty sociable person—after all, you like hanging out with your friends, right? And they seem to like you as well.

But it's different when you have to be charming to a stranger or even to someone you don't like that much. You already know this—think of how much you dread going to a family event, like a wedding, reunion, or piano recital. You know you'll have to talk to great-aunts and second cousins you barely know. You're sure you'll be bored. You hate the idea so much that you do everything you possibly can to get out of it, maybe even pretending to be sick on the actual day.

Instead of complaining to your parents or holding the thermometer over a lightbulb to fake a high fever, you can use that situation to brush up on your spy skills.

Let's take your great-aunt as an example. Imagine you've been seated next to her at the wedding reception. You've both got a plate of food in front of you. And now you're supposed to talk to her.

You look at her for a moment. She's easily a hundred years older than you. She doesn't know the difference between an Xbox and an X-Man. And all you know about her is that she has a cat named Fluffy.

What could you possibly have in common? What could you possibly find to talk about? You may feel like staring glumly at your plate as you begin to plot your escape, but you should actually be feeling very excited—because you're sitting next to the perfect person to help you practice to become a case officer!

Try this: Pretend she's an aide in the government of a foreign country. In fact, she works in the office of the president! You've been assigned to assess her personality and figure out if you could convince her to work with you on secret matters.

That's a pretty hard thing to do! How can you win her over? You need to chat with her, show an interest in her life, and help her relax. You need to be friendly.

So how do you do that? Ask her questions about her life. Maybe you should start with that cat Fluffy.

If you picked the right question, you may find your great-

aunt can talk for quite a long time about all the cute things Fluffy does, the brand of food Fluffy likes best, and Fluffy's favorite sleeping spot. Normally, you would find all this very boring. You might even be tempted to sigh and roll your eyes a little bit, but not now, because you're acting like a case officer who's trying to make friends.

As your great-aunt continues to talk, you need to do your part to keep the conversation going. To do that, really listen to what she says; don't just drift off into a daydream. Nod occasionally or say, "Mm-hmm" to show you're listening. Pick up on something she's just said and ask a question to draw her out further. Sometimes talking can actually be hard work, especially when the person you're with is very shy or nervous. The more you work at it, the better you'll get.

Gradually, as you talk to your great-aunt (or to the person you may want to spy for you), you'll see her drop her guard and become more relaxed. If this were a real situation—if you were really recruiting your great-aunt to steal those secret files—this conversation would probably be just the beginning of the relationship you want to develop. Over the course of months or even years, you would continue meeting. You would remember details about what she's interested in. You might give her a small but meaningful gift, based on what she's told you—a special collar for that cat, perhaps. And then one day, you would ask for a small favor in return . . .

How to Talk to Anyone

Even if you're only chatting for a short time—for example, at dinner or on a plane flight—be genuinely interested in the other person.

Let them do most of the talking.

Never say, "You're wrong." Respect the other person's thoughts, opinions, and ideas.

Try not to argue. Look for bridges of understanding and common interests.

Try to see the other person's point of view.

If you want to ask the person to do you a favor, see if you can lead the conversation so that he ends up thinking it was his idea.

PRACTICE YOUR OBSERVATIONAL SKILLS

Most of our daily routines are so repetitive we rarely notice our surroundings. After all, how many times have you taken the bus to school? How many times have your parents driven you to soccer practice? How many times have you walked down the street to a friend's house?

Hundreds of times, probably. You become so familiar with what's around you that it's easy to let your eyes glaze over. But a spy is always alert and watchful. To develop the spy's way of looking at the world, try this:

Become aware of your surroundings

As you're riding the bus to school, try to remember each house and business you pass. Every day, note any changes you see. For example:

- Does the dry cleaner have a GOING OUT OF BUSINESS sign in the window?
- Is there a moving van parked in front of the blue house?
- Did the man who lives in the yellow house start digging up his yard for a garden? (And if so, what did he plant?)
- Is the same red van always parked in the alley behind the Chinese restaurant—until one day it isn't?
- Did the family at the end of the block get a basketball hoop for Christmas?
- Was the YIELD sign at the corner stolen last night?
- Are there new skid marks on the road that show that a car went out of control in last night's rainstorm?

The more you watch and the more you practice your observation skills, the more you'll see!

Learn to describe someone in ten seconds

What if you happen to spot a criminal on the run, or a suspected spy casing a government building? How well would you be able to describe that person to the police or to the CIA?

One way to get better at describing people is to practice this exercise:

Choose a person next to you who will be your subject.

- Spend ten seconds studying that person.
- Now, look away so you can no longer see the person, and jot down everything you remember. Give yourself two minutes to do this.

Here are some things to look for:

Hair
- Color
- Length
- Texture (smooth, curly, wavy, etc.)

Eyes
- Color
- Style of glasses or sunglasses
- Squinting or apparent difficulty seeing

Skin color

Body type
- Height
- Weight
- Build (slim, skinny, stout, bulky, etc.)

Voice
- Accent
- Volume (booming, soft, average)
- Sound (smooth, rough, cracked, hoarse, melodic, etc.)
- Tone (angry, coaxing, teasing, pleasant, impatient, frightened, upset, sad, etc.)

Clothing

In addition to a general description of the color and style of your subject's outfit, ask yourself:
- Did the clothes look too big or too small?
- Did they look worn or brand-new?
- Were they designer clothes or casual clothes?
- Were there any slogans on the clothes (such as T-shirt mottos or brand logos)?
- Did the colors match or did it look like the subject put on whatever was at hand?
- Were the clothes neat and pressed, or rumpled and dirty?

- What kind of shoes did the subject wear?
- Did they look scruffy and rundown, or neat and polished?
- Did the subject wear jewelry?
- If you were close enough to notice, did the subject wear perfume or aftershave lotion?

Once you've written down everything you remember, look back at your subject and compare your notes with the real person.

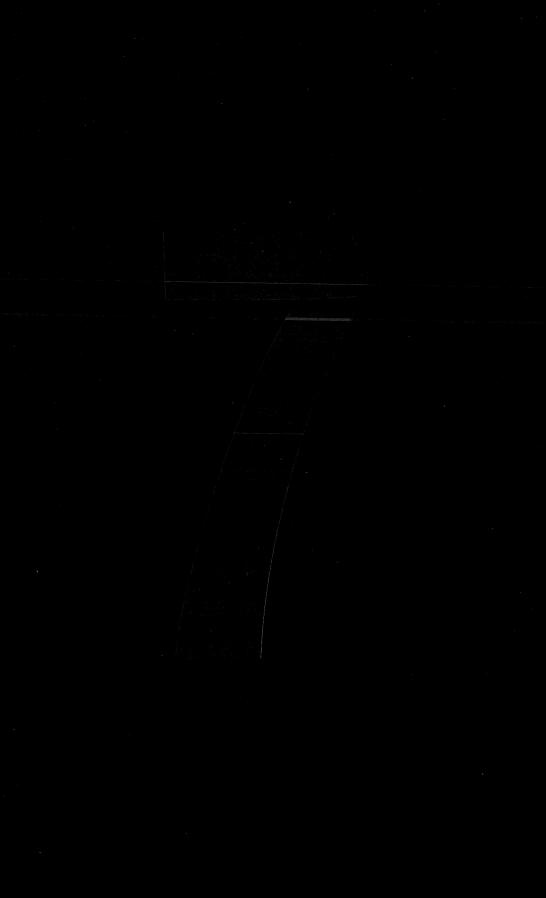

CHAPTER 7

THE FUTURE OF SPYING

fter World War II, the United States and the Soviet Union emerged as the world's two superpowers. They were also adversaries with very different kinds of governments. For the next forty years, they competed with each other for military and political influence in what became known as the Cold War.

When the Soviet Union broke up in 1991, Americans soon realized that now they faced many adversaries, not only one. Instead of the threat of a war with another superpower nation, there were the constant threats of hostile actions by other countries and terrorist groups. As former CIA director James Woolsey said after the Soviet Union collapsed, "We have slain a large dragon, but we now live in a jungle filled with a bewildering variety of poisonous snakes. And in many ways, the dragon was easier to keep track of."

For intelligence, this jungle of poisonous snakes poses serious challenges. Intelligence officers now need to keep track of multiple countries and groups throughout the world, from North Korea to the Middle East, and from international terrorists to global narcotics traffickers. Preventing nuclear terrorism, dealing with biochemical weapons, and thwarting Internet attacks that could paralyze everything from air traffic control systems to the international financial world—these are just some of the tasks confronting the intelligence community today. The end of the Cold War was a victory of sorts, but it did not lead to a more peaceful and cooperative world. In many ways, spying is more critical and challenging than ever.

APPENDIXES

Appendix A

THE INTELLIGENCE COMMUNITY

Get ready for some alphabet soup! Every government agency is known by its official name and its acronym (for example, the Central Intelligence Agency is commonly known as the CIA). If you really want to sound like an insider, learn to refer to these organizations by their initials.

The intelligence community (IC) is made up of sixteen agencies. Fifteen of them report to the sixteenth agency, the Office of the Director of National Intelligence (ODNI, or simply DNI), which was created on the recommendation of the 9/11 Commission. The ODNI is responsible for overseeing the management of personnel and resources within the other fifteen agencies of the IC.

Eight of the agencies are under the Department of Defense (DoD). The other six are under civilian departments. The remaining agency, the Central Intelligence Agency, is not under any other department of government but reports directly to the DNI and the National Security Council (NSC) in the White House.

The eight Department of Defense agencies are:

- National Reconnaissance Office (NRO): Builds and operates the nation's reconnaissance satellites
- National Security Agency (NSA): Makes and breaks codes
- National Geospatial-Intelligence Agency (NGA): Creates topo-graphical maps, publications, and digital products
- Defense Intelligence Agency (DIA): Collects intelligence

through the military attaché cadre abroad and provides analyses
of intelligence for the military

- Air Force Intelligence, Surveillance, and Reconnaissance Agency:
  The intelligence branch of the U.S. Air Force
- Army Intelligence and Security Command (INSCOM): The intelligence
  branch of the U.S. Army
- Marine Corps Intelligence Department: The intelligence branch of
  the U.S. Marine Corps
- Office of Naval Intelligence (ONI): The intelligence branch of the
  U.S. Navy

The six non-DoD agencies are:

- The Department of Homeland Security (DHS), which was created after
  9/11 and merged with several other major government departments,
  such as the Immigration and Naturalization Service and the Coast
  Guard.
- The Federal Bureau of Investigation (FBI), which is part
  of the Department of Justice. It is the premier federal law
  enforcement agency in the United States and has responsibility
  for counterintelligence and intelligence on terrorist threats
  within the United States.
- The Drug Enforcement Agency (DEA), a law enforcement agency
  under the Department of Justice responsible for enforcing drug
  laws in the United States.
- The Bureau of Intelligence and Research (INR), a branch of the
  U.S. State Department that reviews intelligence reporting from
  other agencies to serve the needs of U.S. diplomacy.
- The Department of Energy (DOE), which has four overriding national

security priorities: insuring the integrity and safety of the country's nuclear weapons, promoting international nuclear safety, advancing nuclear nonproliferation, and continuing to provide safe, efficient, and effective nuclear power plants for the United States.

- The Department of the Treasury, the steward of U.S. economic and financial systems and an influential participant in the global economy. It includes an intelligence unit called the Office of Terrorism and Financial Intelligence (TFI).

Intelligence by the Numbers

The U.S. intelligence community employs roughly 100,000 people and has an annual budget of more than $40 billion.

Appendix B
FOR MORE INFORMATION

Books

The Code Book: The Science of Secrecy from Ancient Egypt to Quantum Cryptography, Simon Singh, Anchor, 2000: A useful and well-written history of codes and ciphers.

I Lie for a Living: Greatest Spies of All Time, Antony Shugaar and International Spy Museum, National Geographic Books, 2006: Short, fascinating profiles of spies from biblical days to the present.

International Spy Museum Handbook of Practical Spying, International Spy Museum, National Geographic Society, 2004: A tongue-in-cheek look at the tricks of the espionage trade.

The Master of Disguise: My Secret Life in the CIA, Antonio J. Mendez, Harper Paperbacks, 2000: A behind-the-scenes look at the world of espionage by a former CIA chief of disguise.

Secrets, Lies, Gizmos, and Spies, Janet Wyman Coleman and International Spy Museum, Abrams Books for Young Readers, 2006: A fun overview of the history of espionage.

Spy Book: The Encyclopedia of Espionage, 2nd ed., Norman Polmar and Thomas B. Allen, Random House Reference, 2004: A comprehensive reference book with more than 2,500 entries on everything from famous spies to clever gadgets to spy culture and more.

The Ultimate Spy, H. Keith Melton, DK Adult, 2006: A visual guide to the most inventive and fun spy gadgets that have been made through the ages.

Web sites

Air Force Intelligence, Surveillance, and Reconnaissance Agency:
www.afisr.af.mil
Central Intelligence Agency (CIA):
www.cia.gov
CI Centre:
cicentre.com

Department of Homeland Security (DHS):

www.dhs.gov/index.shtm

Federal Bureau of Investigation (FBI):

www.fbi.gov

International Spy Museum:

www.spymuseum.org

National Security Agency (NSA):

www.nsa.gov

Office of the Director of National Intelligence (ODNI):

www.dni.gov

Office of Naval Intelligence:

www.nmic.navy.mil

U.S. Army Intelligence and Security Command:

www.inscom.army.mil

U.S. Department of Justice:

www.usdoj.gov

U.S. Intelligence Community:

www.intelligence.gov

U.S. Marine Corps Intelligence Department:

hqinet001.hqmc.usmc.mil/dirint/default.html

U.S. State Department Bureau of Intelligence and Research:

www.state.gov/s/inr

Index